mosaics
practical projects for the garden

stylish ideas for decorating your outside space with
25 step-by-step projects

helen baird

BOURNEMOUTH

2005

LIBRARIES

southwater

This edition is published by Southwater

Southwater is an imprint of Anness Publishing Ltd
Hermes House, 88–89 Blackfriars Road, London SE1 8HA
tel. 020 7401 2077; fax 020 7633 9499
www.southwaterbooks.com; info@anness.com

© Anness Publishing Ltd 2005

UK agent: The Manning Partnership Ltd, 6 The Old Dairy, Melcombe Road, Bath BA2 3LR;
tel. 01225 478444; fax 01225 478440; sales@manning-partnership.co.uk

UK distributor: Grantham Book Services Ltd, Isaac Newton Way, Alma Park Industrial Estate,
Grantham, Lincs NG31 9SD; tel. 01476 541080; fax 01476 541061; orders@gbs.tbs-ltd.co.uk

North American agent/distributor: National Book Network, 4501 Forbes Boulevard, Suite 200,
Lanham, MD 20706; tel. 301 459 3366; fax 301 429 5746; www.nbnbooks.com

Australian agent/distributor: Pan Macmillan Australia, Level 18, St Martins Tower, 31 Market St,
Sydney, NSW 2000; tel. 1300 135 113; fax 1300 135 103; customer.service@macmillan.com.au

New Zealand agent/distributor: David Bateman Ltd, 30 Tarndale Grove, Off Bush Road, Albany,
Auckland; tel. (09) 415 7664; fax (09) 415 8892

All rights reserved. No part of this publication may be reproduced, stored in a retrieval system, or
transmitted in any way or by any means, electronic, mechanical, photocopying, recording or otherwise,
without the prior written permission of the copyright holder.

A CIP catalogue record for this book is available from the British Library.

Previously published as part of a larger volume, *Mosaics by Design*.

10 9 8 7 6 5 4 3 2 1

Publisher: Joanna Lorenz
Editorial Director: Judith Simons
Project Editor: Doreen Gillon
Text Editor: Alison Bolus
Designer: Adelle Morris
Production Controller: Pedro Nelson
Additional text: Caroline Suter, Celia Gregory, Mary Maguire, Cleo Mussi, Marion Elliot
Photography: Polly Eltes, Debbi Treloar, Rodney Forte, Spike Powell, Tim Imrie,
Adrian Taylor, Debbie Patterson, Zul Mukhida

Publisher's note

Projects are graded for difficulty from 1–5 indicated by this brush symbol.

The authors and the publisher have made every effort to ensure that all the instructions
contained in this book are accurate and that the safest methods are recommended.
Readers should follow all recommended safety procedures and wear protective
goggles, gloves and clothing at all times during the making of mosaics. You
should know how to use all your tools and equipment safely and make sure you
are confident about what you are doing. The publisher and author cannot accept
liability for any resulting injury, damage or loss to persons or property as a result
of using any equipment in this book or carrying out any of the projects.

Contents

Inspiration

Mosaic is a remarkably durable and versatile medium – you will see it in public places, on the outside of buildings, in the playground or park, and it is a perfect medium for decorating patios and gardens. Beautiful and colourful, mosaics that are created for your enjoyment now, are a legacy for the future.

Contemporary mosaicists work in all manner of styles and bring immense flair to the art. Some draw on traditional influences, while others forge new ground in their use of size, shape and materials.

Modern Mosaics

Mosaics may have a history that reaches back before Roman times, but the inspiration behind the designs can come from the everyday world around us. Designs can be influenced by our surroundings, from people and animal life, to landscapes and art. These influences can affect not just the motifs but also the choice of colour and texture, and the type of materials to be used. All these things will affect the movement and feel of the final piece of mosaic.

Mosaic is now being applied to all kinds of objects in the garden from small nightlight decorations to patio floors and tables, and in this book you can see the effectiveness of mosaic as a hard-wearing design element. Mosaic artists all around the world derive inspiration from many sources, including nature, animal and plant forms, as well as from the repeating or geometric patterns typical of Roman, Celtic and Cubist art. The bold and abstract art of 20th century artists, such as Gaudí, Picasso and Matisse, has also greatly influenced the work of many current mosaic artists. Some employ traditional materials in exciting new ways and others incorporate more unusual materials in their work.

The scale of work varies from small portable panels and accessories to patios and large expanses of floor as well as murals and immense sculptures. Sculptural mosaics are currently very popular among young artists, but many prolific mosaic makers work on panels, murals and outside pieces.

Above: This bright mosaic of blue glazed tile fragments highlights the maritime theme along with sea-washed stones and spiky planting.

Left: This patio floor is mosaiced in different shades of smashed terracotta, and the walls of the flowerbeds are covered in broken blue ceramic tiles.

Opposite: La Via è incerta: a tree poem by Elaine M. Goodwin, a panel which was specifically designed for a quiet, contemplative area of the garden.

The depiction of the human form can take several guises. It can be realistic, as the Romans chose, or it can be more abstract. Likewise, birds, animals and fish can be shown naturalistically or allegorically.

Humans and Animals

Figurative mosaic in the hands of an expert may lend itself to great detail and intricacy. In such mosaics, the contours of the face and body are skilfully rendered through the way in which the tesserae are cut to size and positioned for their shape – notably to show the jut of the chin, cheekbones and brow. Tesserae are chosen to suggest the modelling of the features, for their gradations of colour and tone and to show the way light and shade fall on the face or body.

Ancient Roman images of the living world are mostly realistic, though sometimes they convey a quirky sense of humour. Animals in art have often served a symbolic purpose, for example dogs can indicate fidelity. Birds were a common Roman subject, especially doves at a fountain, which suggested harmony and peace.

In Byzantine times, mosaic was largely confined to religious or imperial subjects and was concerned to show figures such as emperors, Christ, God, the Virgin Mary and the saints in an idealized, and therefore essentially stylized, way. Forms were made slender, elongated and more elegant, faces became regular and expressionless, and gestures and rituals (such as benediction) were formalized and ritualized. It is a style that continues to inspire mosaicists today.

Moving with the times

In later centuries, including the Renaissance and Victorian eras, mosaics remained largely classical and representational in inspiration.

During the 20th century, however, there was a move towards the abstract representation of human figures. This

Above: Cleo Mussi's figures are made of oblong pieces in grid and herringbone patterns. The heads and faces use broken crocks and cup or jug handles for ears.

style of depicting people was practised by many artists, including Pablo Picasso, Matisse and Chagall, whose styles and superb workmanship lent themselves well to mosaic, with the emphasis on outline and colour rather than detail, and the free rendition of line and form.

Modern depiction

The current revival of interest in mosaic often displays a more naturalistic approach, revelling in the beauty and detail of the natural world. Nature can be depicted in numerous ways. For example, a bird could be the main focus within a panel or roundel, or be a stand-alone image on a plain background, such as a garden wall. How the mosaic is executed will depend on the artist's own style. Animals and birds can be treated in a symbolic manner, or they can be allegorical or humorous, realistic or naturalistic. They can appear in outline against a one- or two-colour background, or in silhouette, or have two- or three-dimensional effects. More unusual materials can be added to give detail, texture and depth.

Often animals, birds and insects will form part of a larger mosaic; when they do there needs to be enough tonal contrast in the work to allow the images to stand out, and colours must be chosen carefully. Birds and insects are challenging subjects, but the potential for using vibrant colour is endless, especially with bright plumage. With regard to the human form, today's mosaic artists can choose to depict this in many ways, varying from ethnic art to the vibrant, contemporary approach of the strip cartoon.

Below far left and centre: Takako Shimizu's cobweb and spider brilliantly convey the delicacy and transparency of the web. The well-camouflaged mosaic bat has texture and a three-dimensional quality.

Below: A heron made from materials found on the banks of the River Thames, is sited near Tower Bridge.

The ocean and the teeming variety of life found in it have provided the mosaic artist with a rich source of inspiration for centuries. Likewise, landscapes, whether naturalistic or abstract, appear often in mosaic.

The Natural World

Marine themes are popular choices for bathroom mosaics. Splashbacks, tiled panels, floors and walls can all be decorated with dolphins, fish and shells. The recreation of landscapes will tend to be seen in large-scale mosaics, such as wall panels, or even whole walls.

Marine life

Many mosaic materials, especially the intense and vibrant material smalti, are wonderful for recreating the beautiful colours of fish and the many shades of the ocean – azure, emerald, turquoise and aquamarine. Marine themes offer wonderful opportunities for mosaic artists to experiment with exciting and vivid colour.

Marine life, including dolphins, fish, octopuses, starfish and seaweed, can create a flowing mosaic design, full of action and energy. The impression of water, light and movement can be conveyed effectively and with surprising economy in the way in which the tesserae are laid. Artists can also intersperse the mosaic with iridescent and reflective materials, such as mirror, to highlight certain areas and create a glistening scene.

Mosaics inspired by sea life are often very graphic and highly patterned. In fact, the scales on fish often look like mosaics themselves, and mosaic artists can depict this natural patterning with intricate detail.

Above: A detail from a frame by Norma Vondee, showing a classical-style dolphin. The white tiles highlight an area of the body, making it appear to glisten.

Landscapes

As with any painting, the creation of a landscape begins with the composition. It needs to be planned and sketched out, and the order of work and colours and tones of the tesserae need to be considered in advance.

Landscapes can, at first glance, appear to be faithful to reality, but most will involve a certain amount of stylization, of tidying up, of selecting particular subjects for the foreground and background, of highlighting

Right: A stylized tree mosaic by Elaine M. Goodwin. Perfect when there is no room for the real thing.

Below right: Roman mosaic provided great inspiration for artists throughout the last millennium. This reproduction, using tiny pieces of marble and stone, depicts sea creatures that were intended to look as if they were swimming around a classical water feature.

details and of trying to create a feeling of distance and three-dimensional space. Images are built up by laying lines of regular or cut tesserae around images such as trees or hills, and backgrounds can include other patterns. A mosaic landscape is like a pixellated image that has to be viewed from a certain distance for it to be in focus.

Mosaic landscapes in earlier centuries were often very detailed, showing the subtle undulations of hills, the movement of water and the gradations of blue in the sky, but images do not have to be naturalistic to be effective. Some contemporary mosaic artists take inspiration from naive art and the surreal landscapes of de Chirico, and they have produced scenes that make full use of mosaic's textural and graphic qualities. Such works suggest a complete landscape rather than showing highly detailed images and objects.

For the mosaic maker, plants and flowers are appealing subjects. They soothe the senses, are easy to look at, are universally popular and valued, and can be depicted in many different artistic styles.

Plants and Flowers

Natural plant forms are a very popular theme in mosaic, and plants are often woven into the designs of mosaic borders. They can flow around a panel or large mural, creating wonderful rhythm and activity, which adds interest and depth to a design. Plant forms can be depicted in a very elegant and stylized manner.

Contemporary mosaicists often use the medium's graphic qualities to produce remarkable work based on natural forms. Bold colours and chunky textures can combine to create vivid three-dimensional images. Plants and flowers are also excellent individual images, perhaps best for table tops and panels, as the petals, leaves and stems lend themselves well to flowing ornamentation. Trees, especially the tree of life, are a common theme in mosaic.

The images could be depicted in subtle materials, such as marble, and have delicate, soft-toned flowers, or they could be bold and graphic and less representational, using funkier colours and materials, such as vitreous glass and mirror. Ceramic tiles can give a warm, earthy feel to mosaic pictures of plants.

Left: Tree of Life – *a panel with a border of hand-painted Mexican tiles by Helen Baird. Trees are a popular source of inspiration in mosaic.*

Above: These simple tiles take their inspiration, colour and shape from the bright sunflower.

Above right: Detail of part of the bush from Bird on a Bush, a marble mosaic using soft, warm variegated tones, by Salvatore Raeli.

Right: This garden ornament by Rebecca Newnham shows how well natural plant forms can be expressed abstractly.

Far right: The knobbly textured surface of a pineapple is vividly conveyed by Norma Vondee.

Many mosaics make use of non-representational geometric and abstract patterns of one form or another. The range of motifs is almost limitless, and designs with repeated patterns are ideal for borders.

Geometric and Abstract

By their nature, geometric patterns are very well suited to the art of mosaic. The basic outline is simple and ideal for the shape of tesserae, and shapes can be repeated as often as is needed. The repetition is not monotonous; quite the opposite. The effect can be soothing and pleasing to the eye, and variations can be achieved through different colourways.

Pattern

A repeated pattern is an effective way of linking spaces: for instance, a path and hall floor could both be in a simple chequerboard pattern, the path in, say, black and white, and the hallway in blue and white. The transition from

outdoors to indoors is conveyed by the change in colourway. Although the two areas are relatively small, a continuity of pattern makes the overall space seem larger.

There are many standard geometric patterns to choose from, such as the Greek key, which remains ever popular, the intertwining, flowing rope designs of Celtic art, or the sinuous calligraphic motifs of Islamic or Arabic art. Geometric shapes frequently occur in 20th century art, and the blocks of colour of Mondrian, for example, would translate well into a mosaic project.

Above: Water collects in this beautiful eye-shaped mosaic by Norma Vondee, designed as a decorative feature for a docklands balcony.

Left: A simple repetition of three shapes in the same colours creates a three-dimensional effect in this garden path.

Opposite: Echoes of the art of Paul Klee are visible in this geometric birdbath in tones of blue. The grid effect is offset by the changes in colour.

Design

Once you have your inspiration, next comes the practical part of the design. Before embarking on a project consider its situation and the materials to use in order to make it durable enough to survive. Also the intended use should be taken into account. For instance, a mosaic designed as a flooring will need to be smooth and without edges to trip up on and waterproof so it can be cleaned. All these elements will affect the final design that you decide upon.

The wide choice of materials available means that designing a mosaic is a highly personal process. You need to consider such aspects as size, location, function and colour before starting work.

Practicalities

Left: A dull brick wall is enlivened by an impressionistic mosaic of two cockerels by Takako Shimizu.

All you need to do is be clear about what you want to achieve and how you want to realize it. Do this, and the materials, colour and style will marry happily with setting, mood and size to give you a mosaic of which you are proud. Before committing tesserae to adhesive, consider the following points.

Function

Always consider the main function of the mosaic: is it practical or decorative? Most mosaic is hardwearing and water-resistant, which makes it quite safe to use for floors of a garden room or patio. If the work is to withstand wear and tear from feet or soap and water, think about which materials will be best suited to your needs: glass, for example, is not so suitable for the passage of feet, bikes and perhaps the odd piece of garden equipment.

Location

Consider where the mosaic is to be positioned. Every aspect of the design – whether it is representational or abstract, the size, the colours to be used and also the materials – is influenced by its position in the garden.

When you are designing with mosaic, you have the liberty to use just one material, such as smalti, or to combine as many as you wish. Sometimes, this freedom can make it harder to reach decisions. Of course, no object exists in a vacuum and there will be other factors to consider when creating your designs.

Your mosaic may be intended for a predetermined place within an open-air space, surrounded by other objects. It may also be used for a specific purpose, such as to contain water. Your designs should also take into account the fact that mosaic is long-lasting and the colours virtually permanent. Unlike textile, paper or even paint, stone, glass and ceramic do not disintegrate; nor do they break easily or fade. Once the setting medium has hardened, changes cannot be made. These qualities are the great strengths of mosaic, but they also mean you cannot go over your work and cover it up.

Focal point

Decide whether the mosaic is to stand out from or blend in with its surroundings. Will it be the focal point of a decorative or planting scheme? Your answers will determine how strong the design needs to be.

Size

You need to decide on the size of the mosaic. Ensure that the design is in scale with the overall size: a tiny pattern will look out of place in a large mural, while a big pattern will look just as wrong in a tiny space.

Remember, too, that patterns or designs look larger the closer they are to your eye level. Look at one of the illustrations in this book at eye level, then put the same page on the floor; you will see how much detail is lost. Operate on a "less is more" principle and take out superfluous detail for smaller-scale pieces or those that will be viewed only from afar.

Being so durable means that mosaic is ideal for out-of-doors, where wind, rain and frost would quickly see off a less hardwearing medium. When considering your initial design, make sure your mosaic fits within its environment. Mosaic is a bold medium and you can cover large areas with it and create dramatic effects.

points to consider for EXTERIORS

- What is the mosaic for?
- Where is it going to be sited?
- Do you want it to blend in with established plants and garden features, or will it be the centrepiece from which all else flows?
- Are the colours suitable for its purpose, size and location?
- Is the mosaic the right size for its specific purpose: not so small that it is lost, nor so big that it dominates the space?
- If it is to convey information, such as a house name or number, is the design clear enough and uncluttered with detail to enable it to be viewed from a distance?

Above: The hot colours of this small water feature by Tabby Riley suit the exotic planting around it.

Light

Bear in mind the nature of daylight where you live: blue in temperate areas and more red in tropical parts. Take some tesserae outside to see how natural light alters their colours.

There is no reason why you cannot use strong, hot colours in temperate areas, but be aware of how vibrant they can look. Mosaics in brilliant reds and oranges need to be carefully placed in temperate gardens. If allowed to peep from under lavish green planting, they can add a touch of drama and humour, and are good for shady areas, dark courtyard gardens or a particular "room" in a large garden, perhaps set among hot-toned flowers. Using cool blues and greens in warmer settings can, conversely, create an area of calm.

Siting

Clever positioning is part of a successful mosaic, where all aspects of its design (subject, pattern, framing, colour, texture and size) come together in the right setting. Choose a design that is appropriate for the site.

When you are working outside, consider the view. If the mosaic is to be seen at an angle, make sure it gives the best view. If the piece is in an architectural setting, make sure that the design is sympathetic to its surroundings.

Colour is one of the most fundamental elements of any mosaic design and has a profound effect on our response to the work. In addition, the way light, real or artificial, falls on these colours is hugely important.

Using Colour

When deciding which colours to use, you should have some samples to place in the setting you have in mind. Here you can see how the natural light falls on them. Colour samples should be viewed in all the types of light in which they will be seen and consideration should be given to how the light changes at different times of the day.

Hot and cool colours

What we perceive as colourless white light is divided into the colours of the spectrum – red, orange, yellow, green, blue, indigo and violet. These divide broadly into hot colours (red, orange

and yellow) and cold (green, blue and indigo). The shades that centre around violet (a mixture of red and blue) tend to be cooler or warmer, depending on the proportion of red to blue: mauve and lilac incline to cool, maroon and purple to warm.

In addition, colours are either predominant or recessive: some catch the eye more than others. It is a question not just of light and dark, but of which colours attract the eye first, and which are seen second. So, when deciding which colours to use, you need to bear in mind the visual effect they will have. A palette of warm colours – reds,

oranges and yellows – will create a warm impression. They will also be strong, dominating their surroundings. And because they draw the eye, they will make spaces seem smaller.

The cool colours of blues, greens and indigos, coupled with the "hard" effect of mosaic, may make a cold area seem more so. Along with browns, they are also recessive, so they will be well suited to making small spaces seem larger, provided you do not opt for too many dark tones, which will make areas seem more confined. So, soft blues, greens and lilacs would be a good choice for a mosaic at the end of a small garden.

When it comes to dark and light colours, received wisdom is that a dark area stands out more when surrounded by light-toned colours. This happens if the colours are not too bland. However, it can often be as successful to play up the dark aspect by choosing a similar tone of another colour. The secret is to make the colour deep but rich, such as dark scarlet, blackcurrant, peacock blue or racing green. Boldness pays off. Whichever colour you do choose, note that if using large areas of the same colour, varying the tone and sizes of the mosaic pieces adds interest.

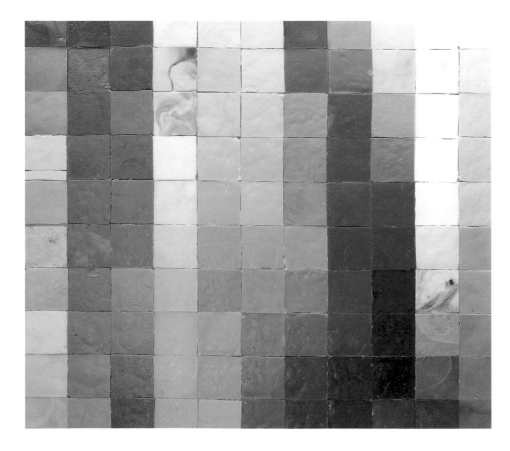

Left: This is a small indication of the vast range of colours and hues of smalti that are now widely available to the mosaic artist.

Above: Using darker and lighter colours throws different elements of a design into relief and brings others to prominence.

Above: A strong colour used against a light background stands out more clearly than white on a coloured background.

Above: The use of colour alone can produce entirely different results from the same pattern.

Also take into account the items or plants that will surround your mosaic. However much you may want it to provide a focal point, it needs to bear some relation to the existing colour scheme in the garden.

Cool and warm light

The fact that the quality of light varies depending on which country you live in becomes particularly relevant when considering the garden. In temperate latitudes, the light, even in midsummer, tends to be blue.

In the Mediterranean and tropical parts of the world, the light is significantly warmer and redder. This explains why the colours of Provence in France, Andalucia in Spain, Italy or Santa Fe in New Mexico – ochres, terracottas and earth tones with splashes of cobalt blues and rust reds – look so right there but do not always translate so well in temperate zones. By contrast, the soft greens, browns and grey-blues that suit cloudy skies can look too subdued and washed-out in stronger sunlight.

White and dark grout

In mosaic, the gaps between the pieces are as much a part of the design as the tesserae themselves, and these gaps are filled by a grouting medium. The effect of the mosaic varies dramatically depending on the colour of grout chosen: a white grout will make the overall effect very much lighter; a dark grout is deep and sombre but can create contrast. It is well worth testing out a small sample to decide which effect you want. See the section on grouting, on page 48.

You can create almost any pattern or shape you want with mosaic, once you have gained some experience of cutting and working with the medium. Outlines, rhythm and variety, and shading are all vital elements.

Using Pattern

If you are a beginner, it is sometimes better to think of mosaic as a medium that is most effective in broader outline rather than fine detail. Pattern alone can be the focus of a mosaic.

Simple outlines

If you can sketch, draw or paint, you may find that your initial attempts at design may not be right for mosaic, as you may be tempted to add too much detail by way of shading. Adopt a "less is more" principle.

Geometric shapes are ideal for creating rhythm in mosaics and they will not become monotonous. Squares or oblongs, checks, chevrons, circles, swirls or spirals, Greek key, interlocking or separated – all are intrinsically pleasing to the eye and have an inbuilt sense of movement. This is why these motifs have remained so popular across the world and through the ages.

If you prefer to adapt an existing design, all you need to do is trace the basic shape, hold it away from your original to make sure the outlines are sufficient to show what you want to portray, then make your outlines the right size.

Left: Arch Air Condensed – *detail of a bee from a recycled china mosaic by Cleo Mussi. The background patterns are as vivid as the bees.*

Top: This detail shows various ways of changing direction and outlining movement.

Below: This mosaic table top by Salvatore Raeli shows how the pattern dictates the direction of the tiles.

Top: Here the pattern is created by the different sizes and shapes of the pieces.

Below: Bold, strong patterns can be made by using larger, clipped pieces of tiles – shape and pattern become one.

Top: The lines here are laid in curves, to give a sense of movement.

Below: This intricate design by Cleo Mussi uses the direction of the pieces to emphasize the pattern.

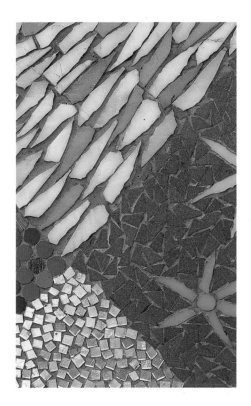

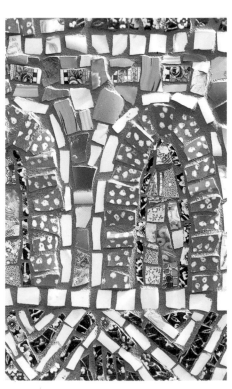

Texture can be one of the most interesting, exciting aspects of mosaic. Even on a flat panel, the depth of tile can vary and many materials can be used to vary the surface and create sparkling shapes and textural schemes.

Using Texture

Different materials have their own inherent qualities. Clay or ceramic have an even surface but have a slight organic roughness. Metal is hard and angular. Wood is rough but warm to the touch. Stone is smoother and cooler in its effect, while smalti and glass are the most responsive to light.

Mixed media

Combining two or more different materials is a way of adding drama, pattern and variety. Mixed media can achieve all kinds of exciting textural effects. Inserting pieces of broken china in an otherwise plain design adds not just colour and pattern: the broken pieces have a different texture and the fractured edges add spots of roughness to the even surface. You can contrast ceramic, which is slightly textured, with glass, which is smooth, or metal with stone. If you experiment

Above: Iridescent, multi-faceted beads, shells and glass all contribute to the varied texture of this dramatic, sculptural garden wall head by Takako Shimizu.

Left: A detail of a mosaiced garden seat, which provides durable external seating, designed by Celia Gregory. The stones make rough, textured breaks in the smoother blue and gold sections of the seating area.

with combinations of various textures, however, do not overload the mosaic with too many at the expense of clarity.

Setting

Textures should be chosen according to the purpose of the mosaic. A garden table should be smooth but a seat or wall mosaic can almost be three-dimensional. Likewise a sculpture covered in mosaic can be as textured as you wish. A patio floor or garden path should not be slippery underfoot, nor should it be so uneven that people risk tripping when they walk on it.

There is also an aesthetic aspect to choice of texture, so that it suits its setting. A rougher texture might look right in a farmhouse yard, but smoothness looks better in a more classical courtyard setting. The hardness of metal is ideal in a contemporary loft-style interior, while stone and pebbles are a natural choice for a garden.

Right: A close-up of Norma Vondee's beautiful panel shows how the artist has depicted the sharp, spiky texture of a pineapple and included ridged glass along with rough and smooth ceramic pieces.

Below: A mosaic octopus clinging to a rock by Takako Shimizu. Its body is decorated with beads.

Materials and Techniques

Mosaic is a versatile art form with great potential for personal creativity, and the range of materials available is visually exciting, colourful and tactile. And, as mosaic becomes more popular, the choice of material continues to grow. Planning projects and preparing the materials carefully enables you to create the mosaics you want, and this is followed by the vital grouting and cleaning stages, after which your mosaic is ready to be displayed.

The subtle colours of marble, the opacity of smalti and the sheer opulence of gold leaf make these invaluable materials. These three types of material give a luxurious appearance to any mosaic.

Marble, Smalti and Gold Leaf

Each mosaic material has its own qualities that will influence the colour, style, look and texture of the finished piece. You can choose to work in just one medium or mix materials to create interesting texture and variety. Marble, smalti and gold leaf can work together to produce sumptuous results.

Marble

This is a natural material; it was used in Graeco-Roman times and is still associated with the luxurious qualities of modern Italian mosaics. Its hard and durable qualities make it excellent for use on floors. Marble is also a subtle material: it represents sheer beauty and natural elegance, and has a depth and timeless quality beyond any other material.

Above right: Marble comes in large slabs that can be cut into squares by hand to produce a more authentic style of mosaic.

Above far right: Smalti has been made for over 2,000 years. It is opaque and creates a wonderfully textural finish to mosaic.

Right: Machine-cut marble in regular squares on mesh or paper backing is effective for covering large areas.

Far right: A selection of tiles with gold and silver leaf twinkle with luxury and magic.

The colours are soft and the variations in tone are subtle: white, chalky pinks and rose, through to delicate greens, blues and blacks. Polishing intensifes the colours. When marble is cut, it has a crystalline appearance and the grains vary according to which part of the world the stone has come from.

For use in mosaics, marble is generally cut from rods with a hammer and hardie (a type of anvil). It is an expensive material, and this limits its use to the finest quality of mosaic.

You can also buy marble that has been machine-cut into regular squares. These squares are laid on to a paper backing, which can be soaked off. The handmade characteristic of the mosaic is lost in this form, but its quality is not impaired, and this is a cheaper form that can be used to cover large areas quickly.

Smalti

Traditionally made in Italy, smalti is opaque glass that is available in a great variety of colours. It is individually made, and the thickness, colour and size vary slightly each time. Each round slab, called a *pizze*, is made from molten glass fired with oxides, metals and powdered marble. Once it has cooled, it is cut into tesserae. It is often sold by the half kilo (1¼lb). *Smalti filati* are threads of glass rods of smalti used for micro-mosaics.

Designs made from smalti have a slightly uneven characteristic that creates a brilliant reflective surface. This bumpiness means that smalti mosaics are often not grouted and cannot be used on floors. Smalti comes in a superb range of colours, and any irregularities create character.

Gold leaf

This is the most opulent tile available to the mosaic artist. It is expensive, yet irresistible, and nothing can surpass its reflective quality. It can be used sparsely in a mosaic and still have a great impact and effect. The tesserae have a backing glass, which is usually

Above: Storing tiles in glass jars is a colourful and practical way to see what you have in stock.

turquoise, yellow or green. Then there is a layer of 24-carat gold leaf, which is protected with a thin layer of clear or coloured glass called the *cartellina*. The gold tesserae can have a smooth or bumpy surface.

Different variations are available with silver or copper leaf, a thin film of gold alloy or other metals. The colours of tile, ranging from deepest gold to vivid blues and greens, are formed when either the *cartellina* or the backing glass is altered.

With their luminous quality, wide range of colours and great choice of surface texture, glass tiles are invaluable to the mosaic artist. Ceramic tiles, which are widely available, offer additional textural variation.

Glass and Ceramic Tiles

These are usually made from vitreous glass and glazed and unglazed clay or porcelain, and come in small, regular tiles. They are laid on to mesh or brown paper to make up sheets measuring approximately 30 x 30cm (12 x 12in), which can be used to cover large areas without the tiles having to be laid individually. The range of materials is always expanding and there is a huge variety of colours and shapes to choose from.

Glass tiles

Vitreous glass is the most commonly used mosaic glass. Its production has been standardized, and it is therefore cheaper than smalti and more accessible to the amateur. It comes in sheets, and the individual tile is a regular square about 2 x 2cm (¾ x ¾in). The

Right: Vitreous glass tiles come on sheets of mesh or brown paper, which are soaked off in warm water. The individual tiles can be clipped into smaller squares.

Above far right: Vitreous glass is a commonly used material; there is a lovely selection of colours. They are easy to clip with mosaic tile nippers.

Far right: Ceramic mosaic tiles come in many shapes and colours, and different kinds of textures.

sheets can be used whole to cover large areas or split into sections for individual mosaics.

Glass is available in a wide variety of colours. The famous Bizzaria range has a grainy quality to the glass and offers a beautiful selection of tiles that have copper blended into the glass, creating a reflective quality that the other tiles can lack. Cutting the individual tiles into four creates the classic square tesserae; the glass is easy to clip and offers extensive potential for intricate design.

There is a now also a new range of glass mosaic made in France. The colours are more rustic than Bizzaria. The glass is smooth and the concentration of the colour is even throughout, appearing like plastic. When these glass tiles are blended with the other glass ranges, they provide the mosaicist with a beautiful palette.

Glass is liable to chip or crack, so tile manufacturers have developed several types of sheet mosaic that are suitable for floors: these are non-slip and non-absorbent and meet many of the regulations associated with commercial properties.

Glass tiles can be shiny, round, square, bumpy, thick, thin, smooth or textured, and come in many different colours. Tiles for mosaic artists are like sweets for children: it is difficult to

know which ones to choose. Stored in clear glass jars, the colourful array can be quite spectacular.

Ceramic tiles
Mosaic ceramic tesserae are round or square and are made from porcelain. They are good for creating texture, as they can be glazed or unglazed: a combination of the two creates surface

Above: Display your mosaic tesserae in groups of colours in clear glass jars. You can easily see what you have available to use, and the gradations of tone and shade.

interest. The colour is uniform in unglazed tiles, and the surface is likely to be matt and more porous than glazed tiles. Ceramic tiles are inexpensive and widely available.

All the materials mentioned so far build an image using mainly squares. Broken-up household tiles, smashed china and mirror and pieces of stained glass, however, create mosaic pictures in a very different style.

Tiles, China, Mirror and Glass

Shiny household tiles, broken pieces of china, in all colours and shapes, pieces of reflective mirror and shimmering stained glass all bring a new creative freedom to mosaic making.

Household tiles

Glazes on household tiles can be shiny, which enables you to play with the reflection of light in the design. When smashed up into irregular shapes, they are fantastic for working into abstract designs. The random shapes of the pieces also make them excellent for covering three-dimensional and sculptured surfaces. They are easy to handle and allow a freedom in expression that some regular square tiles lack, especially when working over curves.

Household tiles can reflect the contemporary aspect of mosaic. They offer enormous variety and versatility to the mosaic artist and it is possible to cover large areas cheaply with them.

China

The use of broken china is a wonderful way to recycle and make something beautiful out of otherwise useless items. A mosaic created with broken china is completely individual because no two pieces are likely to be the same.

China and crockery are not really suitable for intricate designs, but are wonderful for working with patterns

and texture. The curving nature of the material gives the final mosaic a textured finish. Odd pieces of pottery with quirky handles, lids and patterns can add some humour to a mosaic.

Mirror

You can buy mirror in sheets made up of small squares, or rectangles, or in large sheets that need to be smashed up. Mirror works very well scattered through a coloured mosaic. It also produces a fantastic effect when covering entire surfaces, especially sculptured forms. You can generally get offcuts from a glazier for free.

Stained glass

Walking into a stained glass supplier is like walking into an Aladdin's cave.

Above and above left: Plain household tiles are easy and cheap to obtain and can be easily cut to shape. They are good for sculptures and can be useful when you require the mosaic to be water-resistant.

Not only is there the most beautiful array of colours, but the glass has a wonderful shimmering quality to it, rather like beautiful jewels. There is even a stained glass that is iridescent and reflects light like mother-of-pearl.

Some types of stained glass are pieces of art in themselves. They can be used to cover whole surfaces for a luxurious finish or used in small areas to highlight details in a picture or an abstract pattern. Using stained glass in a mosaic design will create something extra special.

Right: The uneven quality of broken cups and plates creates texture, and the patterns and designs are also interesting to play around with in your own designs.

Below and below centre: Stained glass offers a beautiful array of colours and textures, and possesses wonderful reflective qualities. Each sheet of glass could be a piece of art in itself, and when it is broken up into small fragments provides a fantastic mosaic material.

Below far right: Recycling broken crockery to use in mosaic is an inventive and cheap source of materials. Collect pieces, and sort them by colour and pattern.

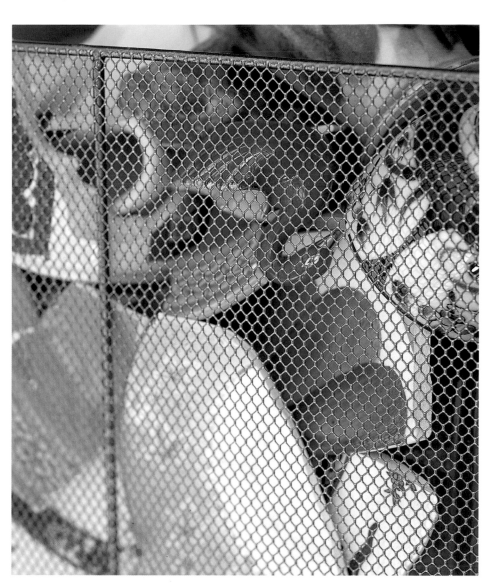

When making decorative mosaics, you can use both traditional materials and more unusual found and collected objects, ranging from shells and washed glass from beaches, to glass jewels and semi-precious stones.

Mixed Media

Using a variety of materials can bring personality and originality to mosaic designs. Mixed materials are particularly effective in sculptural mosaics and for creating a variety of textures and depth in two-dimensional work. It is also fun to gather a collection, such as natural materials from beaches or rivers, or old china from second-hand or thrift stores. There are no boundaries to what can be used, and it can be challenging to experiment with new methods and new materials.

Pebbles

Some of the earliest known mosaics were made from pebbles, and there is still a strong tradition in making pebble mosaics in Greece. In Lindos, Rhodes, you can find many pebble doorsteps and pavements.

Pebbles from the sea or rivers can be found in many subtle colour variations. They have a certain simplicity that is easy on the eye. They are long-lasting and it is possible to seal them, which makes them appear wet and the colours richer. Pebbles are traditionally used to cover large areas in gardens. They offer good drainage, and the simple designs look good without being overpowering.

Left: Glass beads with a flat metallic back used for making jewellery are brilliant for bringing a sparkle to mosaics.

Top: Stone, marble and slate can be cut into small pieces to create natural, subtle yet textural, mosaics.

Top: Small pieces of washed glass can be added to mosaics for effect. Their soft colours give a gentle look.

Top: Glass, plastic and antique beads all work well in mosaics, adding texture and colour to the work.

Above: Shells come in beautiful soft colours and are traditionally used in grottoes or garden follies.

Above: Washed glass and old pottery can often be found on a riverbank. Both will add character to a mosaic.

Above: Pebbles are good for creating simple, lasting designs and have natural muted tones and textural qualities.

Shells

Seashells, in their teeming variety of shapes and colours, have provided inspiration for craftspeople for centuries. The Chinese used mother-of-pearl for inlaying. Shells bedded into lime cement line the grottoes of Italian Renaissance gardens, and 18th-century European country house owners adorned their garden follies with them.

Salvaged materials

The edges of washed glass and pottery that have been smoothed and rounded by years of erosion in the water can be found on beaches and riverbanks. The effect of the water also softens the colours to create a gentle mosaic material. Collected or salvaged materials could include anything from old coins to forks and spoons. Metal foil, building blocks or even dice can be used.

Beads and jewels

Glass beads and jewels catch the light and twinkle. Their unevenness creates texture, which emphasizes the detail in a mosaic. Antique beads often have peculiarities within the glass that make them distinctive. You can buy jewels created for jewellery making that have a flat back, which makes them easier to lay, and placed in a mosaic they will add glints of colour.

Creating a design is fun, and collecting ideas in a scrapbook will be very useful for inspiring your projects. The design will affect your choice of materials, colours and style and the most suitable method of application.

Planning Projects

Take inspiration for your designs from books, magazines, other artists, nature or any other source that stimulates you. Keep any pictures or images that grab your attention for reference later. Stick them in a scrapbook and make notes about what you liked.

Drawings

The initial drawing will be only a guideline for your mosaic. Keep it simple and clear, with strong lines. If you cannot draw, trace an image or cut out a photocopy, and enlarge or adjust it to a suitable size and draw around it. It may be a good idea to make a few copies, so that you can try out different colour schemes before buying the tiles.

When you start applying the tesserae, your ideas may change as you work. This is all part of the evolutionary process of responding to the materials and their colour and texture.

It is not usually necessary to make all the design decisions at the beginning of the project. Creativity is a journey; allow the space during the process for new ideas and additions to unfold. When thinking about your design, bear in mind the colours, textures and contrast of the materials. Also, bear in mind how much time you want to spend on your mosaic, as this may influence the intricacy and complexity of the design.

Starting out

If the task is site specific, make an accurate template with graph paper or brown paper and/or take measurements before you start the detailed planning and work. Make clear notes while you are on site so it is easy to decipher the figures and information gathered when you are in your studio. It may help to photograph the site, too.

If you are a beginner, it is best to start with basic techniques and a small project, such as a pot stand, terracotta pot or small wall panel. As you become more confident, you can be more ambitious and explore your creativity.

Choosing tiles

The appearance of the mosaic is totally dependent on the materials you use. The design may even revolve around using a certain tile, the unique quality of which is your source of inspiration. Discovering how different materials work alone and with each other is an exciting aspect of mosaic artistry that takes time to master.

There is a fantastic range of tiles from all over the world in different colours, glazes and textures. You can use stone, with its soft colours, or choose from a lavish range of stained glass. There is no shortage of choice.

Aside from aesthetic decisions, there are various factors to take into account when choosing. The cost could be a consideration; for example marble is a very beautiful and durable material, but it is very expensive, while porcelain is a much cheaper alternative.

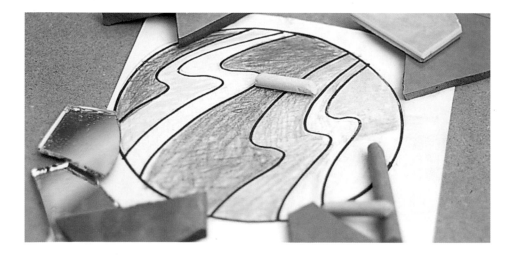

Left: It is useful to make a simple line drawing first using a soft pencil, then emphasize the lines with a black pen and shade in the colours to be mosaiced.

Above: There is a huge range of mosaic tiles to choose from. Vitreous glass tiles, shown here, are best suited to indoor work.

Left: Tile sample boards are a useful way of choosing colours and tiles for a project. Tile suppliers have a wealth of knowledge, and it is important to check with them that the tiles you choose suit the project you are undertaking.

Qualities of tiles

Not all tiles are suitable for all situations, so it is vital to make the right choice if your mosaic is to last. Each tile and material varies, so check their qualities and uses when you buy them.

Glass tiles or stained glass would be damaged quickly if positioned on a floor and exposed to hard shoes. Glazes also come in varying levels of hardness; a soft glaze would restrict the tile use to inside. A harder glaze can be used on the floor, and a frost-proof tile can be used outside. The fired clay that lies under the glaze also has its own individual qualities, such as absorbency, which can affect whether the tiles are suitable for a pond or swimming pool.

choosing the right technique

Each project is different and no task is approached in exactly the same way. You need to decide which technique to use and the suitable fixing agents that are required. Here are some questions that you should consider before starting:

- Where is the piece to be finally positioned?
- Will you work directly, for example on to the pot?
- Will you choose a semi-indirect method, for example on to mesh, which is good for a floor panel?

- Is the site accessible, or is it easier to make the mosaic off-site?
- How durable does the mosaic need to be?
- Does the mosaic need to be water-resistant, waterproof, weather- or frost-proof?

While a small project could be made in the kitchen, it is advisable to allocate a special space in which to work, giving you a clean area for drawing and a workbench or table for doing the mosaic.

Creating a Workspace

The workspace is your own creative environment, so some wall space should be allocated for displaying your finished mosaics and any images that inspire you. Shelving will be needed, to store books, files, tools and materials, and a water supply is essential.

Posture

The most comfortable way to mosaic is definitely working at an easel or a table. It is important to have the seat or stool at a suitable height. It is worth spending time getting this right so that a good posture can be maintained and you can avoid shoulder and back strain.

Lighting

Ideally, the table or workbench should be placed near a natural source of light. Daylight is the best way to see true colour. When light is limited or when you are working at night, daylight bulbs are ideal. It is best to have more than one light source to avoid shadows.

Storage

When organizing materials, it is a good idea to build shelving and store tiles in glass or clear plastic jars, so it is easy to see how much stock you have and all the different colours. Tools are expensive and rust easily, so keep them clean and dry. Adhesives and grouts solidify if they get wet, so they must all

be stored in a damp-free area, preferably in sealed containers. Most chemicals have a limited shelf life and can go off, so should be checked regularly.

Large mosaics

When working on a mosaic that is too big for a table or easel, you should work on, or at least prepare the design on, the floor. You will need a hard

Left: Larger projects can be planned on the floor or in an area where it is possible to see the whole design.

safety

These are sensible precautions you can take to avoid injuring yourself:

- Wear goggles when cutting materials to avoid getting fragments in your eyes. Hold the mosaic tile nippers away from your face.
- Wear a face mask when cutting wood or mixing powder to avoid inhaling fine powder into sinuses and lungs.
- Wear hardwearing gloves when cutting wire and use rubber or latex gloves when mixing up powders, and also when grouting, cleaning or sculpting. Your hands

will get dry and sore if they come into contact with water and adhesives for too long. It is also recommended to wear thin latex gloves when making mosaics. Take care, and keep antiseptic cream, plasters and hand cream on your shelving.

- Hold mosaic tile nippers at the far end of the handle to avoid hand blisters.
- Always clean and vacuum the work area regularly to avoid an unnecessary build-up of dust.
- Create your mosaic with awareness to the safety of those around you, as well as yourself.

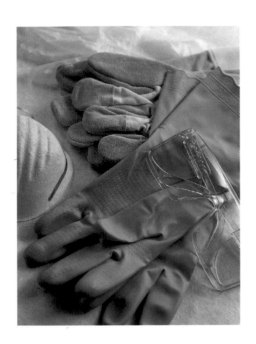

surface, so if the floor is carpeted, use a large piece of wood. If you are using mesh or brown paper, you should draw up the design and get a clear understanding of the whole image. Then you can cut the image into fragments and work in sections on the workbench.

If you need to see the whole design develop, it is best to work on the floor and protect the surrounding surfaces with plastic sheeting. This can be hard on the back, so you should take regular breaks and have a good stretch.

Preparing for work

Once you have chosen where and how to work and what to mosaic, you should gather all the required tools and materials together, mix enough fixing agents for the immediate work

and prepare a good range of tiles before commencing.

Keep the work area clean, sweeping away loose fragments regularly. It also makes good sense to keep coloured tiles in some kind of order, placing different tiles, colours and shapes in separate small piles, for ease of use. When working with cement-based adhesive, clean off any excess while it is damp; if left overnight, the cement will harden and become very difficult to remove from the surface it is on.

Cleaning up

Sweep up or vacuum at the end of each session, as fragments get everywhere and can be sharp. Cleaning and reorganizing will also make the next day's work much easier. If different

Above: Good light, a work surface and seating at the right height for good posture are essential for comfortable and productive mosaic making.

Above left: Gloves, goggles and face masks should be worn to protect against any injury or harmful inhalation caused by sharp chips or ground glass or tile.

cement-based adhesives and grouts are allowed to mix in the drains, this can cause serious blockages and endless problems. When cleaning mixing bowls that held these materials, therefore, always scrape out and throw away as much excess as possible, before washing away the residue. Placing gauze over the plug can avoid the need to clean the drains regularly.

The materials for a mosaic usually need some form of preparation for the work. Tiles can be smashed, nipped or sawn, glass cut and marble or smalti reduced to the correct size pieces by a hammer and hardie.

Preparing Materials

By preparing and clipping the materials you will be using before you start the mosaic – in the same way as a painter would mix a palette of paints – you will be free to concentrate on laying the mosaic design.

Sheet mosaic

Many mosaic tiles come on sheets, either on fibreglass mesh or on brown paper; the tiles are about 2cm (¾in) square and the sheets are approximately 30cm (12in) square. These are useful for laying a large area.

When making smaller mosaics using sheet mosaic, you should take the tiles off their backing. To remove the tiles from sheets formed with brown paper or mesh, soak the whole sheets in clean warm water. When the glue has dissolved, the tiles will slip off the backing material easily.

Smashed ceramic tiles

Antonio Gaudí is famous for his extensive use of mosaic in his fairytale buildings in Barcelona. They are very colourful and predominantly use ceramic tiles smashed into small fragments. Ceramic tiles come in an enormous range of colours, tones, textures and glazes, and are suitable for both interior and exterior use, as many are frost-proof. They are fun and easy to work with.

Clipping tiles

Mosaic tile nippers are the essential tool for any mosaicist, and are good for clipping most materials. With practice, intricate shapes can be achieved.

The mosaic nippers should be held at the end of the handles for the best possible leverage. The rounded side of the head is placed over the tile, which need be inserted only a few millimetres. To cut the tile in half, the nippers are positioned in the centre of the tile with the head pointing in the direction the cut is needed. Holding the opposite edge of the tile between thumb, fore-

finger and index finger will stabilize it. The ends of the handles are then presssed together.

Goggles are essential, as initially the tiles seem to fly all over the place. With practice, however, it becomes possible to control the cuts, and the fingers support the bits in place. If the cut goes astray, the excess can be nibbled away on the edge of the tile.

Cutting and sawing tiles

A hand tile cutter is the tool traditionally used for cutting tiles, and it is available from do-it-yourself stores. It

smashing ceramic tiles

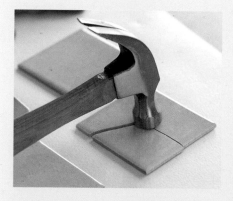

1 Wearing goggles and protective gloves, smash the tiles with a small hammer, aiming at the centre of the tile. To make these fragments smaller, gently smash with a hammer in the centre of each fragment.

2 Pieces can fly all over the place if you hit the tile too hard, so for protection, cover the tiles with a cloth and wear goggles. Use the mosaic nippers to shape the ceramics into the size and style required.

Right: Glass and mirror can be cut with a glass cutter. The surface is scored lightly, using a metal rule as a guide, then broken.

Far right: A hammer and hardie are used to break thick materials, such as stone and smalti, into pieces.

will cut straight lines on tiles, though its use is limited to ceramic tiles with a soft clay base.

Hard floor tiles or stone need to be cut with a wet tile saw. This specialized piece of equipment is essential for certain tasks, such as cutting thin strips of marble, which are then made into the correct size for mosaicing with a hammer and hardie. It is possible to hire wet tile saws.

The saw cuts the material with a metal disc that is revolved by a motor and kept cool with water. As the tile hits the blade, the water can spray out, making this quite a messy but effective technique needing protective clothing.

Cutting glass

A glass cutter is used for cutting straight lines or large shapes in stained glass and mirror.

Right: (from the top) Tile cutters, for cutting straight lines; a tile scorer; mosaic tile nippers, for cutting tiles into shapes; a craft (utility) knife; and a glass cutter for cutting glass and mirror.

The surface should be scored lightly with the cutter, then the ball of the cutter used to tap the underside gently; it will crack along the line. Tile nippers are good for making smaller cuts and detailed shapes.

Goggles and gloves should be worn when handling glass and mirror, since even the smallest splinters cut easily.

Cutting stone and smalti

A hammer and hardie are the traditional tools for cutting stone and smalti, both of which are too thick for modern tile clippers. The material is held over the chisel between the thumb and forefinger and the hammer swung down on to this point. With practice, accurate cutting is obtained.

Mosaics can be laid on to a variety of different surfaces, and, as long as the correct procedures are followed, they will be hardwearing and waterproof and have a professional-quality finish.

Preparation and Fixing

Traditional mosaics were laid on to a cement bed. Now, we can also mosaic on to all sorts of different surfaces, such as wood, old furniture, plaster, ceramic, terracotta or fibreglass.

Bases

Unless working with a sculptured form, you should work on to a flat, even surface for a professional-quality mosaic. Uneven surfaces should be sanded down. If working on to cement, a new surface should be laid; self-levelling cement is an easy option.

The base or surface should be rigid. Any mosaic laid on a flexible surface will lift up if there is movement. So a thin layer of wood should be cut to fit and screwed in evenly to cover the entire surface.

Wood is a very good base, but for an outdoor mosaic or one that will come into contact with water, the wood must be exterior grade, such as marine ply.

Priming surfaces

Most working surfaces, such as wood, concrete, terracotta urns, old furniture or plaster, are porous, so the surface must be sealed with diluted PVA (white) glue (see box below). This greatly improves the sticking power of adhesive and makes the final mosaic more hardwearing and waterproof.

Before sealing, it is important to ensure that the surface is clean of all loose debris and hair. Smooth surfaces, such as wood or fine plaster, should be scored with a sharp implement, such as a bradawl or craft (utility) knife. On more slippery surfaces, such as plastics or existing tiles, a special two-part resin primer can be brushed on to provide a key. It creates a surface to which an adhesive can easily attach.

Diluted PVA glue can also be used to coat terracotta pots in order to make them frost-resistant.

Fixing methods

Once the surface has been properly prepared, there are various ways to fix the tiles. Choosing which technique to use depends partly on where the mosaic is situated and partly on personal preference. The direct method involves placing the material straight on to the working surface. The indirect method involves creating the mosaic off-site, then installing it. Two semi-indirect methods are worked on to paper or mesh off-site and then fitted into the cement on-site, so combining aspects of both methods.

Traditional stone and smalti mosaics were laid straight on to a bed of cement. Modern materials, however, are often much thinner, and need to be stuck as well as embedded.

priming wood

1 Take a craft (utility) knife and score the surface of the wood, creating a key. This improves the grip between the tiles and the adhesive.

2 Mix up PVA (white) glue with water in a ratio of 1 part glue to 3 parts water. Apply this evenly with a dense sponge or a paintbrush.

Right: You will need some, if not all, of these tools to prepare surfaces and apply adhesive. Clockwise from top left: hard bristle brush, paintbrush for glue, notched trowel, hammer, chisel, flexible knife, dustpan and brush, rubber spreader and adhesive applicator.

Direct method

This method involves simply sticking the tesserae, face up, on to the base, which has been covered with a layer of cement-based tile adhesive. It is good for working on to wood or sculptured forms, when working with smashed ceramic tiles, washed glass, tiles of different heights, or when covering large areas. It is also good to work directly into adhesive because it avoids having to spend extra time fitting and allows the design to develop in the environment where the mosaic is situated.

The direct method is easiest to start with and recommended for beginners.

Indirect method

Originally, this technique was devised as a way of making large-scale mosaics off-site, so that they could be moved ready-made, then laid in position. The design would be sectioned into manageable areas, and each area made into a slab. It is equally useful, however, for mosaics that cannot be laid directly due to an awkward location.

working with cement-based tile adhesive

1 Mix white cement-based tile adhesive with water in the ratio of 2½ parts powder to 1 part water, until you have a smooth consistency. Choose and prepare the tiles you are going to use. Apply adhesive to the base with a flexible knife.

2 Stick the tesserae into the adhesive, ensuring good contact by pushing them in with your fingertips. If you use too much adhesive, the excess will squeeze through the gaps and get messy, but if you use too little, the tesserae will fall off.

A wooden frame is made to the size of the finished slab, and greased internally with petroleum jelly. The mosaic is appplied to a piece of brown paper marked with the dimensions of the slab, using the semi-indirect brown paper method (see right).

When the tesserae are dry, the frame is placed over the paper and dry sand sprinkled over the design and nudged into the crevices with a soft brush. The frame is then filled with mortar. The surface is smoothed, then covered with damp newspaper and polythene (polyethylene) sheeting and left to dry slowly for five to six days.

When the mortar is dry, the slab and frame are turned over and the brown paper dampened with a wet sponge, then peeled away. The frame is unscrewed and the slab removed.

Brown paper method

This reverse technique involves gluing the tesserae into position off-site, then setting them into adhesive on-site, cutting up the sheets of mosaic if needed.

When using this technique, the tesserae are glued face down on brown paper with PVA (white) glue; if they are uneven in any way, the irregularity will occur on the underside of the mosaic, making this method ideal for mosaics requiring a smooth surface.

The front of the mosaic is invisible during the design process, so this method is limited to tesserae that are coloured right through.

Once the mosaic sheet is pressed into the waiting adhesive, and been left to dry for 24 hours, the brown paper is soaked off with a wet sponge.

Mesh method

In this second semi-indirect method, fine-weave fibreglass mesh acts as a perfect base for the mosaic. The tesserae are stuck face up on to the mesh, so it

the direct method using PVA glue

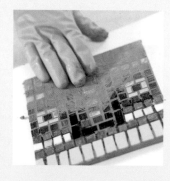

1 Cut a piece of wood to the desired size. Clip a selection of tiles into quarters and halves. Experiment with the tesserae; the design does not need to be complicated.

2 Once you are happy with the design, use a small brush to apply the PVA (white) glue to the back of the tesserae, and stick them in place and leave to dry.

3 Mix up some grey powder grout with water in the ratio of 3½ parts grout to 1 part water. Apply with your fingertips, wearing rubber (latex) gloves.

4 Wipe down the surface with a damp sponge to remove all traces of grout on the tesserae. Once the grout is dry, polish the tiles with a dry, soft cloth.

Left: The completed mosaic, on its brown paper base, needs to be cut into sections that can be handled easily.

is possible to see the mosaic design developing and taking shape. If the mosaic is large, it can be cut up and transported easily. When the tesserae are secure on the mesh, it is pressed, face up, into the adhesive and left to dry.

Cement-based tile adhesives

There is a vast range of modern cement-based tile adhesives for use on both direct and indirect mosaics. They come in a variety of shades, mainly white and grey. Your choice of colour will be influenced by what colour you want to grout in: grey for grey, black or dark colours; white for lighter shades.

Medium-strength adhesive comes in tubs ready-mixed, which is fine for decorative pieces or if the mosaic does not need to be particularly waterproof.

Most large tile companies have their recommended range of cement-based adhesive and additives. It is worth asking which materials are most suitable for the job you are undertaking. There is a variety of products for all situations, from exterior frost-proof, cement-based adhesives through to flexible liquid additives, such as admix, which can be added for extra protection against movement or to make the adhesive suitable for a shower.

PVA glue

This is good for sticking tiles directly on to wood, when it should be used undiluted. For priming or sealing, dilute PVA (white) glue 3:1 with water. It is water-based, so its use is limited to internal use only. It dries slowly, so tiles may be repositioned.

Epoxy resin glue

This is a strong glue made up of two separate components: the hardener and the resin. It is good for use in underwater locations or in damp places, but it has a limited working time and is sticky and toxic, so a face mask should be worn. Epoxy resin glue is useful when working with the direct method as it sets in just four hours, reducing drying times drastically.

Right: This soft mesh is used for subtle relief work, while chicken wire is more effective for larger-scale sculpting. Big exterior sculpting can be formed with bricks or breezeblocks (cinderblocks) then covered with a layer of tile adhesive.

Far right: In the mesh method, the mosaic pieces are glued, face up, straight on to the fibreglass mesh.

Grouting is incredibly satisfying: it unifies the mosaic and blends the images and colours. Designs that felt garish or too busy are softened, and patterns that work with movement come to life.

Grouting

On a practical level, grouting is when the gaps between the tiles are filled with a cement mortar that has a different quality to the adhesives. The process strengthens the mosaic and makes it waterproof. Grouting ensures that mosaic can be a functional art form that can be used in swimming pools, showers, water features, external wall murals or lavish floors.

Grout comes either ready-mixed or in a powder and in a variety of colours. There are also powdered stains that you can add to create almost any colour you want. The colour you choose will have a profound effect on the colours and look of the finished mosaic. Some of these differences can be seen in the four panels below. The grid of grey grout overpowers the neutral tiles, and the white grout is also very strong. The cream grout works well with the white tiles, as there is balance, while the beige grout warms the white tiles.

Note that white grout will blend with pale tiles, lighten darker colours and contrast blacks, while black grout will deepen blacks and blues, make reds and greens really rich and contrast with white. The qualities and varieties are endless, giving you great scope for creativity.

Grouting is a messy job, especially if stains are used, so clothes and surroundings should be well protected and rubber (latex) gloves should be worn to protect the hands.

When to grout

The finished mosaic should be grouted when the tile adhesive is dry. Before

Right: These four panels of neutral vitreous glass mosaic were grouted in four different shades: clockwise from top left, beige, grey, cream and white.

Below: Grout comes in different colours, which can dramatically alter the finished look of the mosaic.

being grouted, small mosaics can be gently shaken to remove loose adhesive, and any loose tiles can be re-adhered. On larger-scale mosaics, light vacuuming can be effective.

On a large-scale project, the whole surface should not be grouted in one go, because when you start to clean off the grout, the first areas may have already dried. One section should be grouted at a time, then cleaned off before the next section is begun. The grout should be left to dry for 24 hours until it is completely hard.

Above: For grouting and cleaning your mosaics, you will need a mixing trowel, a grout spreader, some cleaning cloths, a sponge, a bowl and protective sheeting.

Above: Wear rubber (latex) gloves and grout your mosaic using a rubber spreader. Rub the grout into any gaps using your fingertips.

grouting and cleaning

1 When the mosaic is being laid, adhesive can squeeze through the gaps between the tesserae. Scrape this away with a blade or craft (utility) knife. Then ensure that the mosaic is clean.

2 Wearing rubber (latex) gloves, mix together the powdered grout and clean water in a bowl. Follow the manufacturer's instructions to achieve the right consistency.

3 Apply the grout over the mosaic, using your fingers, a grout spreader or a rubber spreader. Push the paste into the gaps and smooth it evenly over the whole surface.

4 Wipe away any excess grout with a damp sponge. After 10 minutes, any remaining excess grout can be rubbed away easily with a dry cloth. (If left much longer, remove with a nail-brush or paint scraper.)

Once the colours and the design of the mosaic have been revealed by the cleaning process, attention must be paid to where and how to present the finished work, how to light it and how to maintain its beauty.

Finishing Your Work

If the tesserae of the mosaic have a shiny glaze, the grout will have come off easily with the sponging process. Matt porcelain, however, holds the grout, making it harder to clean.

It is possible to buy an acid called patio cleaner, used by builders for cleaning cement off brickwork. When diluted with warm water, it is very effective for removing resilient grout. If sponged or poured on to the mosaic, it will make a fizzing noise as it eats away at the grout left on the surface of the tiles. After a few minutes, the dirty water can be sponged away. Resistant areas can be removed with a paint-scraper or abrasive paper (sandpaper), before being polished with clean cloths.

Sealing

Stone and pebbles look richer when sealed, appearing slightly wet and retaining their subtlety of tone without the addition of a varnish or shine to the surface. Sealants come in matt or shiny varieties.

Beeswax can be rubbed on to matt tiles to give them a deeper colour. Terracotta tiles need to be treated with linseed oil. This is flammable, so always dispose of cloths that the oil comes into contact with carefully.

Siting

There are no hard-and-fast rules about where to site your mosaic; it is a matter of judgement and common sense,

which you must learn to trust. Asking someone to hold the mosaic in place so you can have a look is always wise. You can usually tell when the site is right. If you are unsure, you can swap with your helper to ask their opinion.

Aside from the positioning of the mosaic, the colour of the surrounding walls must be taken into consideration. You do not want the walls to clash with the mosaic, or for them to overpower it.

Hanging

A small mosaic can be hung like a picture, using wire and picture hooks. Hanging a larger, heavier mosaic, however, requires more thought.

Far left: This colourful panel is lightened by the white grout, and the glazed tiles laid in a Gaudí-style mosaic have a fresh flowing feel. To clean, first spray the mosaic with glass cleaner. Any proprietary window cleaner will do. If you do not have this, use some water with vinegar added to reduce smearing.

Left: Polish with a clean dry cloth, preferably a lint-free one, and you should achieve a good shine on the glass and the glazed ceramic tiles. The colours weave into each other, while the mirror and glass balls make shimmering focal points within the mosaic.

It is important to find out whether the wall you intend to fix the mosaic to can hold the weight. Plasterboard (gypsum board) will not, so if it is a partition wall, the mosaic must be fixed to a supporting strut. When fixing into brick or plaster, you will need to drill holes, using a drill bit that is compatible with the size of screw you have chosen. The correct position for the fixings should be marked on the wall with a pen. Wall plugs (plastic anchors) should be placed in the drilled holes to give the screws something to grip on to, then the mosaic can be hung in place.

Mosaic panels can also be fixed to the wall with mirror plates. Protruding mirror plates are fitted to the wood at the edge of the panel and then the mirror plates are screwed to the wall. Those with a keyhole opening are fitted to the back; they then slot over screws inserted into the wall.

Lighting

Mosaics nearly always look their best in natural light, with its soft tones. Yet the night-time light is important and needs consideration.

A mosaic could be lit with a spotlight fixed in the ground or on a patio. It is important not to over-light and bleach out the colours and subtle reflective quality of the tiles. Different colours and wattages of bulb, as well as different angles and distances, should all be tried.

Maintenance

The best way to maintain a mosaic is to clean it regularly, so avoiding the build-up of resilient dirt. Although this is not so important for outdoor mosaics. A floor mosaic should be swept and mopped with a gentle cleaning agent, making sure the dirty water is removed properly. Decorative mosaics should be dusted and cleaned using glass cleaner and a dry cloth.

Above: These are some of the tools you may need when siting and installing your mosaic. Clockwise, from top right: saw, hammer, abrasive paper (sandpaper), wire (steel) wool, U-shaped hooks, pliers, screwdriver, picture wire, picture hooks, hanging hooks, screw eyes, screws, wall plugs (plastic anchors) and eraser.

If the mosaic has got really dirty, the patio cleaner referred to opposite should be used, though it may be necessary to re-grout after cleaning. If the correct maintenance steps are taken, the mosaic could last for a millennium.

Projects

Garden ornaments are not just the frippery that they are made out to be. Often they are useful objects that we need to have around the garden, but that can be disguised or decorated in such a way as to make them a pleasure to have around. Even those objects which are solely decorative do perform a psychological function in brightening up our everyday lives. All the projects have been graded from one to five, one being the easiest.

Only the most minimalist of gardeners wishes to exclude any suggestion of ornament from their garden. Containers, in particular, are an ideal choice for mosaic and provide a welcome splash of colour in any garden.

Ornaments

Mosaic seems quite at home in a garden, adding a touch of colour to a dull area, or providing a dramatic focal point. Blue colour schemes are ideal to complement the surrounding green.

Pots and containers

Mosaic can be applied to many kinds of garden containers, from night lights, window boxes and chimney pots to the largest urn. The most commonly covered containers are, however, ceramic pots. Use a frost-resistant terracotta pot as a base where you can, and if it is not glazed, you must varnish the inside to stop moisture seeping through from

the inside and pushing off the tesserae. This is important if the pot is to be used for plants that are left outside. It is also advisable to use water- and frost-resistant cements and grouts.

There is also a wide range of excellent plastic containers available that accurately replicate almost any kind of finish you care to name, from verdigris, terracotta and copper to stone, but have the advantage of being lightweight. Mosaic can be applied to add detail and personalize any of these types of pot. Once a pot is covered in mosaic, no one will know that the base is plastic rather than terracotta.

An elaborately carved or shaped antique-style container, in real or simulated stone, may need a different treatment to simple plant pots. Large urns look good partially covered with mosaic, as it highlights the contrast between the pot and mosaic, but tesserae should be chosen to enhance the base colour. Urns make stunning focal points and add a sculptural feel to any garden.

Considerations to take into account concern the appearance of not only the container but also the plants. Your design and chosen colour palette should complement the environment. For example, a restrained geometric design would suit a clipped topiary box tree, but a more vibrant, abstract design would harmonize with bright red geraniums.

Surroundings

In any garden, the plants must be the first feature. You do not want any decoration to "shout" at the plants or detract from their beauty. When planning your design, therefore, you must make the surrounding plants your first consideration, so that your mosaic design echoes their beauty.

Left: A bright urn, and accompanying birdbath, with strong colours and designs are ideal for dark or shady courtyards.

Above top: This garden planter, by Celia Gregory, was made using bricks, shaped with cement and covered with smashed royal blue ceramic tiles. Stones decorate the top of the planter.

Above: In a predominantly green space, brightly patterned ceramic pots by Cleo Mussi add interest.

Above right: This traditional garden urn is decorated with unusual modern faces in subtle, muted tones.

Which plants are going to be nearby and what colours are their leaves or flowers? The leaves may change colour when young in spring, at their peak in summer and when they turn in autumn. If leaves drop, what other plant will then be thrown into prominence? In winter, how does your garden change? Or perhaps your colour scheme is subdued, with grasses and low-maintenance shrubs or evergreens. In this case, do you want ornaments to blend in or stand out?

Out of doors, even under cloudy skies, light is ever-changing and so very important. Will your mosaic be in shade, dappled shade or full sun? What does it look like under different weather conditions, from bright sun to rain?

For all these considerations, you need to choose whether you want to keep to gentle shades and natural tones or opt for bold, bright colours that have impact. Either way, mosaic will complement the natural surroundings and allow your plants to shine.

One jar is used as the base and another is broken into fragments that are painted with stained-glass paints. These fragments are then stuck on to the base jar and the gaps between the glass are grouted.

Jam Jar Night-light

You will need

2 jam jars
Old tea towel
Goggles
Protective gloves
Hammer
Scrap paper
Newspaper
Reusable adhesive
Stained-glass paints
Paintbrushes
Solvent-free, rapid setting
transparent epoxy resin
White cellulose filler
Grout spreader
Scourer
Sandpaper
Acrylic paint

1 Wrap one of the jars in an old tea towel. Wearing goggles and protective gloves, and covering your hair, smash the jar with a hammer. If the jars are of different sizes, smash the larger one. Pick pieces to use as tesserae. Place them on scrap paper with the sharp edges facing downwards to avoid cutting yourself. Wrap any unused glass in newspaper and dispose of it carefully.

2 Use reusable adhesive to pick up the broken pieces of glass and turn them over so that the sharp edges face upwards. Paint the concave surface of each fragment with stained-glass paint. Here, three colours are used. Leave the pieces to dry.

3 Glue the dry painted glass fragments to the base jar, using a transparent rapid-setting epoxy resin, which must be solvent-free. Leave the jar to dry thoroughly.

4 Spread cellulose filler over the surface. Make sure all the gaps are filled. Smooth into the top and bottom edges of the jar and wipe off most of the excess. Leave to dry. If cracks have appeared, use more filler.

5 When dry, clean any excess filler with a scourer and water. Use sandpaper to neaten the top and bottom edges. Colour the filler with acrylic paint.

A mosaic door plaque adds a distinctive touch to your home and will withstand all weathers. Plan the design carefully so that you have space between the numbers and the border to fit neatly cut tesserae.

Door Number Plaque

You will need

Scissors

Craft paper

Floor tile

Pencil

Metal ruler

Vitreous glass tesserae: turquoise, black and yellow

PVA (white) glue

Glue brush

Tile nippers

Cement-based powdered grout

Notched spreader

Sponge

Cement-based tile adhesive

Lint-free cloth

1 Cut a piece of craft paper the same size as the tile. Mark the border and number in reverse on the shiny side of the paper. The border is one tessera wide. There should be room between the border and numbers to insert a quarter-tessera neatly.

2 Dilute the PVA (white) glue to a 50/50 solution with water. Glue the flat sides of the turquoise tesserae on to the border of the craft paper, with a single black tessera at each corner of the plaque.

3 Cut some black tesserae with the tile nippers to make rectangles. Glue the black rectangles flat-side down over the paper numbers.

4 Cut the yellow tesserae into quarter-squares. Lay them around the straight edges of the numbers, using the tile nippers to cut to size as necessary. Glue them flat-side down as before. Place quarter-square yellow tesserae all around the curved edges of the numbers, cutting as necessary.

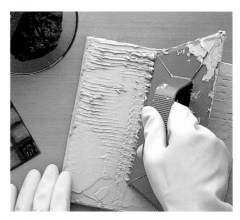

5 Mix the grout according to the manufacturer's instructions. Grout the mosaic with the notched spreader, removing the excess with a damp sponge. Leave to dry. Spread a layer of tile adhesive over the floor tile and key (scuff) with the notched edge of the spreader.

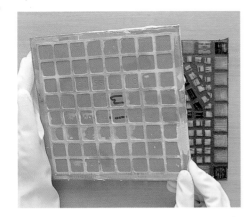

6 Place the grouted mosaic paper-side down on a flat surface. Place the floor tile on top, matching corners and edges. Press the tile down, wipe away excess adhesive and leave to dry.

7 Using a sponge and water, soak the paper on the front of the mosaic. Leave for 15 minutes.

8 Lift one corner of the paper to see if it comes away cleanly. If it does, peel the paper off carefully. If it proves difficult, leave it to soak a little longer and then try lifting it again.

9 Carefully wipe away any surplus glue. Re-grout the plaque, including the sides. Remove excess grout with a damp sponge, then polish the surface with a dry, lint-free cloth.

This unusual and decorative dragonfly plaque is made from plywood and pieces of old china. Search market stalls and junk shops for old plates and saucers, and check your cupboards for rejects.

Dragonfly Plaque

You will need

Tracing paper

Pencil

5mm (¼in) thick plywood, 50cm (20in) square

Jigsaw (saber saw)

Bradawl

PVA (white) glue

Paintbrush

Acrylic primer

Abrasive paper (sandpaper)

Dark green acrylic paint

Cable strippers

Electric cable

Wire cutters

Selection of china

Tile nippers

Tile adhesive

Coloured tile grout

Brush

Cloth

1 Draw a simple design for a dragonfly on to the plywood. Cut out the design using the jigsaw (saber saw) and make two small hanging holes at the top of the body with a bradawl. Seal the front with diluted PVA (white) glue and the back with acrylic primer. When dry, sand the back and paint with green acrylic paint. Strip some electric cable and cut a short length of wire. Push this through the holes from the back and twist together securely.

2 Cut the china into regular shapes using tile nippers. Dip each piece into tile adhesive, scooping up a thick layer, and press down securely on the plywood to fill in the design. Leave to dry overnight.

3 Press coloured grout into the gaps between the china. Leave it to dry for about 5 minutes, then brush off the excess. Leave for another 5 minutes, then polish with a cloth. Hang with suitable fixings.

As well as protecting your table top, this mosaic pot stand will brighten up any meal time. The geometric shape is integral to the pattern in which the brightly coloured tesserae are laid.

Pot Stand

You will need

12mm (½in) thick chipboard (particle board), 30 x 30cm (12 x 12in)

Pencil

Ruler

PVA (white) glue

Paintbrush

Jigsaw (saber saw)

Abrasive paper (sandpaper)

Ceramic household tiles: yellow, dark blue and lilac

Tile nippers

Mirror

Tile adhesive

Flexible knife

Black tile grout

Grout spreader

Sponge

Felt

Scissors

Soft cloth

Clear glass polish

1 Carefully mark the proportions of the pot stand on to the piece of chipboard (particle board); use a ruler to make sure the lines are straight.

Prime both sides of the chipboard with diluted PVA (white) glue and leave to dry. Cut around the outline of the design using a jigsaw (saber saw). Sand down any rough edges and prime with diluted PVA glue. Leave to dry.

2 Using tile nippers, cut the tiles into small pieces that will fit inside the shapes you have drawn. Here, small pieces of mirror have been added to the dark blue sections, and small pieces of the dark blue tiles have been included in the lighter areas. Fix them in position with tile adhesive, using a flexible knife. When the surface is covered, sponge off any excess adhesive and leave to dry for 24 hours.

3 Fill the gaps between the tesserae with black tile grout. Rub the grout into the sides of the stand as well, then leave to dry for about 10 minutes. Wipe off any excess grout with a sponge, then leave to dry for 24 hours. Paint the sides of the pot stand with diluted PVA glue. Cut felt to size and stick it to the back of the stand with PVA glue. Finish by polishing the top with a soft cloth and clear glass polish.

This design relies on the various effects that are created by the juxtaposition of colours and textures. It can quite easily be adapted but should be kept simple for the best effect.

Mosaic Bottle

You will need

Wine bottle

Silicone sealant

Pencil or pointed stick

Vitreous glass tesserae, including white

Tile nippers

Cement-based tile adhesive

Mixing container

Soft cloth

Sandpaper (optional)

1 Clean the bottle, rub off the label and dry thoroughly. Dab silicone sealant on to the bottle using a pencil or pointed stick to form a simple line drawing, such as a series of swirls.

2 Cut white vitreous glass into small pieces, about 2mm/¹⁄₁₆in and 4mm/⅛in, using tile nippers. Stick these tesserae to the lines drawn in silicone sealant, then leave overnight to dry.

3 Choose an assortment of colours from the vitreous glass and cut them into quarters. Some of the quarters will have to be cut across the diagonal, so that they can fit snugly between the white swirls. Stick these to the bottle in a series of bands of colour with the sealant. Leave overnight to dry.

4 Mix up some cement-based tile adhesive and rub the cement into the surface of the bottle. Make sure all the crevices between the tesserae are filled, otherwise the tesserae are liable to pull away, as the silicone sealant will remain rubbery. Wipe off excess cement with a dry soft cloth and leave overnight to dry.

5 If any of the tile adhesive has dried on to the surface of the tesserae, sand the bottle down. For a really smooth and glossy finish, polish the bottle with a dry soft cloth.

Fragments of plain and patterned broken tiles have been incorporated into the design of these plant pots. Collect your materials by looking in junk shops for old china in contrasting and complementary patterns.

Plant Pots

You will need

Terracotta flower pots

PVA (white) glue and brush (optional)

Acrylic paint

Paintbrush

Chalk or wax crayon

Plain and patterned ceramic tiles

Tile nippers

Tile adhesive

Flexible knife

Tile grout

Cement stain

Cloth

Nailbrush

Soft cloth

1 If the plant pots are not frost-resistant and are intended for outdoor use, seal them inside and out with a coat of diluted PVA (white) glue. This will help to keep out any water that might seep into the pourous pot, making it vulnerable to frost damage. Allow to dry.

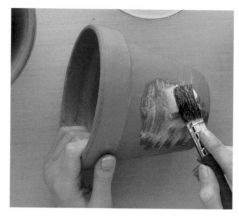

2 Paint the inside of the pots with acrylic paint in your chosen colour. Leave to dry. Using chalk or a wax crayon, roughly sketch out the design for the tile pieces on the unpainted outside of the pot. Keep your designs as simple as possible and in keeping with this small scale.

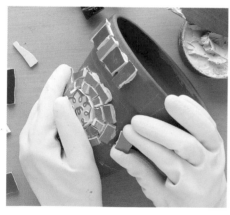

3 Using tile nippers, snip small pieces of tile to fit within your design. Using a flexible knife, spread tile adhesive on to small areas of the design at a time. Wearing rubber (latex) gloves, press the tesserae in place, working on the outlines first, then the background. Leave for 24 hours.

4 Mix the tile grout with a little cement stain. Spread the grout over the pot with a cloth, filling all the cracks between the tesserae. Wipe off any excess grout. Allow the surface to dry thoroughly.

5 Brush off any dried-on grout with a nailbrush. If there are stubborn parts of grout that will not come off at first, you might try wire (steel) wool, a paint scraper, or patio-cleaner. Allow the mosaic to dry thoroughly for at least 48 hours, then polish with a dry, soft cloth.

If you would like to introduce mosaic to an outdoor setting but are daunted by a large project, these tiles are the perfect solution. They can be left freestanding or be fixed to a wall as an interesting feature.

China Tiles

You will need

Plain white ceramic household tiles

PVA (white) glue

Paintbrush

Pencil

Selection of china

Tile nippers

Tile adhesive

Acrylic paint or cement stain

Tile grout

Nailbrush

Soft cloth

1 Prime the back of a plain tile with diluted PVA (white) glue using a paintbrush and leave to dry. Draw a simple, rough design on the back of the tile using a soft pencil.

2 Using tile nippers, cut a selection of china into small pieces that will fit into your design and arrange these in groups according to their colour and shape.

3 Dip the tesserae into tile adhesive and press them, one by one, on to the tile, using the drawing as a guide. Make sure there is enough adhesive on the tesserae; when they are pressed on the tile, glue should ooze out around them. When the tile is covered, leave it to dry overnight.

4 Mix acrylic paint or cement stain with the tile grout. Rub the grout into the surface of the mosaic with your fingers, making sure all the gaps between the tesserae are filled. Leave to dry for 10 minutes.

5 Scrub the surface of the tile with a stiff nailbrush to remove all the excess grout, which should come away as powder. When clean, leave the tile to dry for 24 hours. Finish by polishing it with a dry, soft cloth. Repeat for any other tiles you want to make.

These mosaic spheres can be used for a game of boules, as garden ornaments, or a bowlful could make a striking table centrepiece. Select fragments of china to complement your tableware or garden.

Decorative Spheres

You will need

10 polystyrene (Styrofoam) balls or wooden spheres

PVA (white) glue

Paintbrush

Pencil

Selection of china

Mirror

Tile nippers

Tile adhesive

Vinyl matt emulsion (flat latex) or acrylic paint

Dark tile grout

Nailbrush

Soft cloth

1 Seal the polystyrene (Styrofoam) or wooden spheres with diluted PVA (white) glue. Leave to dry. Roughly draw a simple design on to each sphere using a pencil. A combination of circular motifs and stripes works well, but you can experiment with other geometric shapes and abstract designs.

2 Cut the china and mirror into pieces using the tile nippers. Combine different sizes of tesserae to fit the design. Stick them to the spheres with tile adhesive. Leave to dry overnight.

3 Add a little coloured vinyl matt emulsion (flat latex) or acrylic paint to the tile grout. Wearing rubber (latex) gloves, rub the grout into the surface of each sphere, filling all the cracks between the tesserae.

4 Leave for a few minutes until the surface has dried, then brush off any excess grout using a stiff nailbrush.

5 Leave to dry overnight, then polish with a dry, soft cloth. Allow the spheres to air for a few days before you arrange them.

A plain terracotta pot is decorated with squares of brightly coloured tesserae and mirror glass, set in white tile adhesive. This project is simple but effective – you could decorate several matching pots.

Jazzy Plant Pot

You will need

Small terracotta plant pot

Yacht varnish

Paintbrush

Vitreous glass mosaic tiles

Tile nippers

Mirror

Tile adhesive

Flexible knife

Sponge

Abrasive paper (sandpaper)

Soft cloth

1 Paint the inside of the terracotta plant pot with yacht varnish. Leave to dry. Cut the glass tiles into neat quarters using tile nippers. Cut small squares of mirror to the same size, also with tile nippers. Continue cutting the tiles until you have enough tesserae, in a variety of colours, to cover your pot completely.

2 Working from the bottom of the pot, spread a thick layer of tile adhesive over a small area at a time using a flexible knife. Press the tesserae into the tile adhesive in rows, including the pieces of mirror. Leave to dry overnight.

3 Rub some more tile adhesive all over the surface of the mosaic. Fill any gaps in between the tesserae, then wipe off the excess adhesive with a damp sponge before it dries. Again, leave to dry overnight.

4 Use abrasive paper (sandpaper) to remove any lumps of tile adhesive that may have dried on to the surface of the tesserae, and to neaten the bottom edge of the pot.

5 Smooth some more tile adhesive all over the rim of the pot. Leave until completely dry, and then polish the finished mosaic with a dry, soft cloth.

A terracotta planter can be embellished with pieces of tile, which are further enhanced by being grouted in a colour chosen to complement them. If the planter is frost-resistant, it can safely be used outdoors.

Decorative Planter

You will need

Ceramic mosaic tiles in several colours

Tile nippers

Notched trowel

Tile adhesive

Terracotta planter

Putty knife

Tile grout

Cement stain

Rubber spreader

Nailbrush

Soft cloth

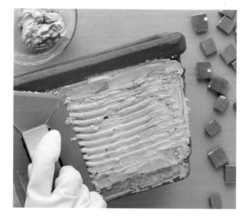

1 Snip the tiles into small pieces with tile nippers. You will need a selection of small squares of a single colour to create the borders, and random shapes in several different colours to fill the space between them. Use the notched trowel to apply tile adhesive generously to the sides of the planter.

2 Using a putty knife, apply a small amount of tile adhesive to the back of the single-coloured square tesserae. Position them on the planter to form two straight lines parallel with the horizontal sides of the planter, making a border at the top and bottom edges of your pot.

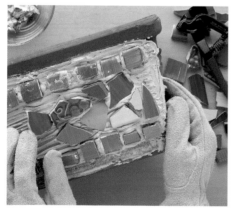

3 Fill in the central design in the same way with the randomly cut tesserae, mixing the colours to make an abstract design. Leave fairly large gaps of a consistent size between the tile pieces, as thick bands of coloured grout are part of the final design. Leave to dry for 24 hours.

4 Mix the tile grout with a little cement stain. Using the rubber spreader, apply grout all over the surface of the planter, pressing right down between the tesserae. Wipe the spreader over the surface of the planter to make sure the grout is evenly applied. Allow the surface to dry.

5 Brush off any excess grout with a nailbrush, then leave to dry for 48 hours. Polish with a dry, soft cloth.

For this flowerpot, which combines both the functional and decorative qualities of mosaic, Cleo Mussi has chosen a design and colours that reflect the flowers to be planted in it. Squares of mirror add reflections.

Part-tiled Flowerpot

You will need

Ready-glazed, high-fired
terracotta flowerpot

Chalk or wax crayon

Selection of china

Tile nippers

Tile adhesive

Flexible knife

Tile grout

Cement stain

Nailbrush

Soft cloth

1 Draw a simple design on the pot, using chalk or a wax crayon. Cut appropriate shapes from the china using tile nippers. Use tile adhesive to fix the tesserae to the pot, spreading it with a flexible knife. Work first on the main lines and detailed areas, applying the adhesive to small areas at a time so you can follow the lines of the design.

2 Fill in the larger areas of the design using tesserae in a plain colour. When these areas are complete, leave the pot to dry for 24 hours.

3 Mix the tile grout with a little cement stain, then spread the grout over the pot with your fingers, filling all the cracks between the tesserae. Allow the surface to dry, then brush off any excess grout with a nailbrush. After the pot has dried for about 48 hours polish it with a dry, soft cloth.

This sunflower mosaic is simple to make, and, if you have enough china, you could make several plaques to brighten up an outdoor wall using bright fragments of china in a harmonious blend of colours.

Sunflower Mosaic

You will need

5mm (¼in) thick plywood sheet

Pencil

Coping saw or electric scroll saw

Abrasive paper (sandpaper)

Bradawl

Electric cable

Wire cutters

Masking tape

PVA (white) glue

Paintbrushes

White undercoat

China fragments

Mirror strips

Tile nippers

Tile adhesive

Tile grout

Cement stain

Nailbrush

Soft cloth

1 Draw a sunflower on the plywood. Cut it out with a saw and sand any rough edges. Make two holes in the plywood with a bradawl. Strip the cable and cut a short length of wire. Push the ends of the wire through the holes from the back and fix the ends with masking tape at the front. Seal the front with diluted PVA (white) glue and the back with white undercoat.

2 Using tile nippers, cut the china and mirror strips into irregular shapes. Dip each fragment in the tile adhesive and stick them to the plywood. Scoop up enough of it to cover the sticking surface; the tile adhesive needs to squelch out around the edge of the mosaic to make sure that it adheres securely. Leave the adhesive to dry thoroughly overnight.

3 Mix some cement stain with the grout. Press small amounts of grout into the gaps on the mosaic with your fingers. Leave to dry for about 5 minutes, then brush off any excess with a nailbrush. Leave again for 5 minutes and then polish well with a dry, soft cloth. Leave overnight to dry.

These little star-shaped wall motifs have been created by Cleo Mussi to add sparkling focal points to a garden. They are particularly effective when displayed in clusters or surrounded by lush foliage.

Star Wall Motifs

You will need

3mm (⅛in) thick plywood sheet

Pencil

Set square (triangle)

Ruler

Pair of compasses

Coping saw or electric scroll saw

Abrasive paper (sandpaper)

PVA (white) glue

Paintbrushes

Bradawl

Wood primer

White undercoat paint

Gloss or matt (flat) paint

Wire

Wire cutters

Adhesive tape

Selection of china

Mirror

Tile nippers

Tile adhesive

Tile grout

Cement stain

Nailbrush

Soft cloth

1 Draw a star motif on a sheet of plywood, using a pencil, set square (triangle), ruler and pair of compasses.

3 Make two small holes through the star using a bradawl.

2 Cut out the star using a coping saw or an electric scroll saw. Sand down any rough edges, then seal one side with diluted PVA (white) glue.

4 Paint the unsealed side with wood primer, then undercoat and finish with a coat of gloss or matt (flat) paint. Allow each coat to dry before applying the next.

▶

5 Cut a short length of wire and bend it into a loop for hanging the star. Push the ends through the holes in the star from the painted side and secure them to the front with adhesive tape.

6 Snip the china and mirror into small pieces using the tile nippers, then arrange these tesserae into groups according to colour and shape.

7 Stick the china and mirror tesserae to the surface of the star, one piece at a time. Take each tessera and dip it into the tile adhesive, or paint some on with a brush, making sure enough is on the tessera to ooze a little from under its edges when pressed on to the base. Cover the surface of the star in this way, then leave overnight to dry.

8 Mix the desired quantity of grout with some cement stain. Wearing rubber (latex) gloves, rub the grout into all the gaps between the tesserae. Leave to dry for a few minutes.

9 Using a nailbrush, gently remove all the excess grout. This should brush away as powder; if it does not, the grout is still too damp, so leave to dry for a few more minutes before brushing again.

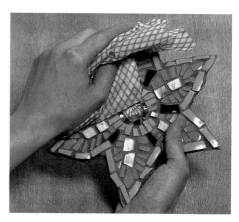

10 Polish the surface with a soft, dry cloth, then leave to dry for 24 hours before hanging outside.

This unusual garden urn is decorated with modern faces but has a look reminiscent of Byzantine icons. Many people shy away from attempting to draw the human form, but such a simple, naïve drawing is worth a try.

Garden Urn

You will need

Large frost-resistant urn

Yacht varnish and paintbrush (optional)

Chalk

Vitreous glass mosaic tiles in various colours

Tile nippers

Tile adhesive

Flexible knife

Sponge

Abrasive paper (sandpaper)

Dilute hydrochloric acid, safety goggles and rubber (latex) gloves (optional)

Soft cloth

1 If the urn is not glazed and it is to stand outdoors, paint the inside with yacht varnish to stop moisture seeping through from the inside and pushing the tesserae off. Leave to dry.

2 Divide the pot into quarters and draw your design on each quarter with chalk. The design used here depicts four different heads and shoulders. Keep the drawing very simple, sketching just the basic elements of the face.

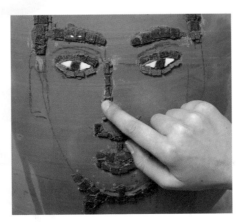

3 Choose a dark colour from the range of vitreous glass tiles for the main outlines and details such as eyes and lips. Snip the tiles into eighths using tile nippers. Spread tile adhesive with a flexible knife and stick the tesserae to the lines of your drawing.

4 Select tiles in a range of colours for the flesh tones, and snip them into quarters.

▶

5 Working on a small area at a time, apply tile adhesive to one of the heads and shoulders and press the tesserae into it. Use a mixture of all the colours, but in areas of shade use more of the darker tesserae, and in highlighted areas use the lighter ones.

6 Repeat step 5 for the other heads, then choose colours for the area surrounding the heads. Spread these out on a clean table to see if they work together. A mixture of blues and whites with a little green was chosen here. Snip the pieces into quarters.

7 Working on a small area at a time, spread tile adhesive on to the surface and press the glass tesserae into it, making sure the colours are arranged randomly. Cover the entire outer surface of the urn, then leave to dry for 24 hours.

8 Mix up more tile adhesive and spread it over the surface of the mosaic with your fingers. Do this very thoroughly, making sure you fill all the gaps between the tesserae. This is especially important if the urn is going to be situated outside. Wipe off any excess adhesive with a sponge, then leave to dry for 24 hours.

9 Use abrasive paper (sandpaper) to remove any adhesive that has dried on the surface of the mosaic. If the adhesive is proving hard to remove, dilute hydrochloric acid can be used, but you must wear goggles and rubber (latex) gloves and apply it outside or where there is good ventilation. Wash any acid residue from the surface with plenty of water. Leave to dry. Polish with a dry, soft cloth.

10 Finish by rubbing tile adhesive over the lip and down inside the pot. This prevents the mosaic from ending abruptly and gives the urn and mosaic a more unified and professional appearance.

Mosaic works extremely well on furniture in the garden. A chair is perhaps not the first item that you might think of applying mosaic to, but would make a real focal point for any patio area.

Furniture

Adding mosaic is a wonderful way to revive tired or battered pieces of garden furniture, and it will also make pieces more weather-resistant.

Tables

A garden table is an ideal subject for mosaic. Not only is it a flat, horizontal surface, and therefore easy to work on, but it, and its surrounding chairs, will often be the centre of attention on the patio or lawn, making it the perfect place to create a dramatic design.

Geometric designs can make an impact by contrasting with the flowing lines of flowers and trees that surround them, while designs inspired more directly by nature can complement their surroundings. Whatever the design or colours used, a mosaic can transform the most humble garden table of any size or shape.

Chairs and benches

White plastic garden furniture cannot be made into works of art, but a simple kitchen-style chair or a standardized garden bench are both ideal candidates for the mosaic treatment.

Right: An old chair is given a new lease of life by the addition of mosaic. A large, three-dimensional object such as this will require a deceptively large amount of tesserae to cover it.

Almost any part of a chair or bench can take mosaic, though you must always remember that they are for sitting on and leaning against, so the mosaic must be flush, smooth and even.

Preparation

Think carefully about the amount of mosaic materials required: covering a large table top or an entire chair (or even a set of chairs) will take a large amount of tesserae.

The element of unity is also important. There should be continuity of pattern or colour to avoid the end result looking disjointed. Pieces do not need to be identical, but they must have some strong visual factor linking them, such as colour or pattern.

Below: A quirky sea urchin seat stands invitingly on the lawn. Vitreous glass tiles are suitable for outdoor use.

Above: This outstanding table is encrusted with scallop, cockle, cowrie, snail, mussel and limpet shells, plus a sea urchin.

Below: Ceramic floor tiles were used to create the star design on this table, and tiny gold tesserae were placed in the large gaps.

The bold design of this table top and the simplicity of its metal frame combine to create a table that would look good in the conservatory or garden. Tiny chips of gold-leaf smalti create glinting highlights.

Star Garden Table

You will need

2cm (¾in) thick plywood

Pencil

String

Drawing pin (thumb tack)

Jigsaw (saber saw)

Abrasive paper (sandpaper)

PVA (white) glue

Paintbrush

Tape measure (optional)

Selection of ceramic floor tiles

Tile nippers

Tile adhesive

Flexible knife

Sponge

Piece of sacking (heavy cloth)

Hammer

Gold-leaf tiles

Soft brush

Plant mister

Dilute hydrochloric acid, goggles and rubber (latex) gloves (optional)

Metal table frame

Screws

Screwdriver

Soft cloth

1 Follow the instructions for the Shades of Blue Garden Table (see page 92) to cut a circle from the plywood. Then prime with diluted PVA (white) glue, paying special attention to the edges.

2 Draw a simple design on the table top. You may need to use a tape measure to get the proportions right, but don't be too rigid about the geometry, as a freehand approach suits this method of working.

3 Cut the floor tiles that are in your outlining colour into small pieces using tile nippers. Try to cut them into a variety of shapes, as uniform shapes would jar with the crazy-paving effect of the smashed tesserae used for the rest of the table.

4 Using a flexible knife, spread tile adhesive around the edge of the table top. Firmly press the outlining tesserae into the adhesive, making sure they do not overlap the edges.

▶

5 Apply tile adhesive to the lines of your drawing and press in the outlining tesserae. Use a sponge to wipe away any large bits of adhesive that have squashed out from under the edges of the tesserae, and leave to dry overnight.

6 Cover the remaining tiles with a piece of sacking (heavy cloth) and smash them with a hammer. Apply tile adhesive to small areas at a time and press in the tile fragments between the outlines of the table top. Do this carefully, as the finished surface must be as flat as possible. Leave to dry overnight or while working on another area.

7 Using a flexible knife, smooth tile adhesive on to the edges of the table. Cut gold-leaf tiles into tiny, irregular tesserae using tile nippers. Place these in the larger gaps between the broken tiles on the table top. If necessary, first insert a blob of tile adhesive to ensure that the gold is at the same level as the tiles as the surface should be flat and smooth. Leave to dry overnight.

8 Spoon tile adhesive powder on to the surface of the table and smooth it into all the gaps with a soft brush. Spray water over the table. When the powder has absorbed enough water, wipe away any excess with a cloth. If the adhesive sinks when wetted, repeat this process. Leave to dry for 24 hours.

9 Turn the table top over and rub tile adhesive into the plywood on the underside with your fingers. Leave to dry overnight. Clean off excess adhesive with abrasive paper (sandpaper). Alternatively, use dilute hydrochloric acid, wearing goggles and rubber (latex) gloves, and apply it outside or where there is good ventilation. Wash any acid residue from the surface.

10 When clean, turn the table top face down on a protected surface and screw the metal frame in place using screws that are no longer than the thickness of the plywood. Finally, polish the table top with a dry, soft cloth.

With a little work and imagination, this battered old chair has been transformed into an unusual, exciting piece of furniture. This example shows the extremes to which mosaic can successfully be taken.

Crazy Paving Chair

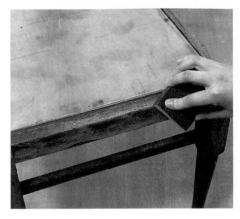

You will need

Wooden chair

2cm (¾in) thick plywood sheet and jigsaw (saber saw) (optional)

White spirit (paint thinner)

Abrasive paper (sandpaper)

PVA (white) glue

Paintbrush

Wood glue

Tile adhesive

Admix

Flexible knife

Pencil or chalk

Large selection of china

Tile nippers

Dilute hydrochloric acid, goggles and rubber (latex) gloves (optional)

Soft cloth

1 If the chair you have chosen has a padded seat, remove it. There may be a wooden pallet beneath the padding that you can use as a base for the mosaic. If not, cut a piece of plywood to fit in its place.

2 Strip the chair of any paint or varnish with white spirit (paint thinner) and sand down with coarse-grade abrasive paper (sandpaper). Then paint the whole chair with diluted PVA (white) glue to seal it.

3 When the surface is dry, stick the seat in place with a strong wood glue. Use tile adhesive and admix (mixed to the manufacturer's instructions) to fill any gaps around the edge. This will give extra strength and flexibility.

4 Draw a design or motifs on any large flat surfaces of the chair with a pencil or chalk. Use simple shapes that are easy to work with.

5 Select china that has colours and patterns to suit the motifs you have drawn. Using tile nippers, cut the china into the appropriate shapes and sizes for your design.

▶

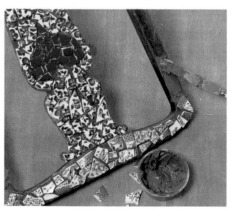

6 Spread the adhesive mixture within the areas of your design and press the cut china firmly into it. Select china to cover the rest of the chair. As you are unlikely to have enough of the same pattern to cover the whole chair, choose two or three patterns that look good together.

7 Cut the china into small, varied shapes. Working on small areas at a time, begin to tile the rest of the chair. Start with the back of the chair first, moving on to the legs, and finally the seat.

8 Where one section of wood meets another, change the pattern of the china you are using.

9 Cut appropriately patterned china into thin slivers and use these to tile the edges of any thin sections of wood. Here, the edges of the back rest are covered. Leave for at least 24 hours to dry completely.

10 Mix up some more tile adhesive and admix. Using a flexible knife, smooth this into the four corners of every piece of wood. Use your fingers to rub it over the flat surfaces. Work on a small area at a time and try to clean off most of the excess as you go. Leave overnight to dry.

11 Sand off the excess adhesive. This can be quite a difficult job, as there are many awkward angles. Alternatively, dilute hydrochloric acid can be used, but you must wear goggles and rubber (latex) gloves and apply it either out-side or where there is good ventilation. Wash any residue from the surface with plenty of water and, when dry, polish with a dry, soft cloth.

Sea urchins are found clinging to wild, rocky shorelines or nestling in rock pools. Their simple, pleasing shapes bring a taste of the ocean to your garden. They come in many colours, including these soft blues.

Sea Urchin Garden Seat

You will need

4 whole breezeblocks (cinderblocks) and 1 small cut piece

Sand

Cement

Hammer

Cold chisel

Charcoal

Vitreous glass mosaic tiles

Tile adhesive

Black cement stain

Notched trowel

Tile nippers

Slate

Piece of sacking (heavy cloth)

Glass baubles, silver and glass circles or stones

1 Mix 3 parts sand to 1 part cement with some water. Use this mortar to join the breezeblocks (cinderblocks) into a cube formed from two L shapes, with a cut block in the centre.

2 When the mortar is dry, knock off the corners of the blocks with a hammer and cold chisel. Continue to shape the blocks into a flat dome, with the cut block at the top.

3 Using charcoal, draw a curved line on each side of the cube to give the impression of a rounded sea urchin. Draw lines radiating out from the centre. Keep your choice of colours simple and bold. Lay out the design before you start and apply the tiles to check the spacing. Vitreous glass tiles were chosen because of their suitability for outdoor work. Cut them into strips for easy lines or soak them off the mesh.

4 Add a small amount of black cement stain to the tile adhesive and trowel it directly on to the surface of the block, no more than 5mm (¼in) thick. Place each tile on the surface of the adhesive and tap it down sharply, once only, with the tile nippers. Do not adjust the tiles too much or they will lose their adhesion. Wrap the slate in a piece of sacking (heavy cloth) and break into pieces with a hammer.

5 Avoid making any sharp edges, as these will have to be filed down afterwards. Use just one dark shade of tiles for the curved line marked in step 3 to give the design visual clarity. Place the broken slate pieces on the adhesive around the square base of the seat and tap them down with the tile nippers.

6 In between the gaps on the square base of the seat, place glass baubles, silver and glass circles, blue and white cut tiles or stones in the pattern of running water. Leave to dry completely. Grout the seat with sand, cement and black stain mixed with water. Allow to dry slowly but thoroughly. To secure the seat in position, dig out a shallow base for two breezeblocks, and then mortar the seat to them.

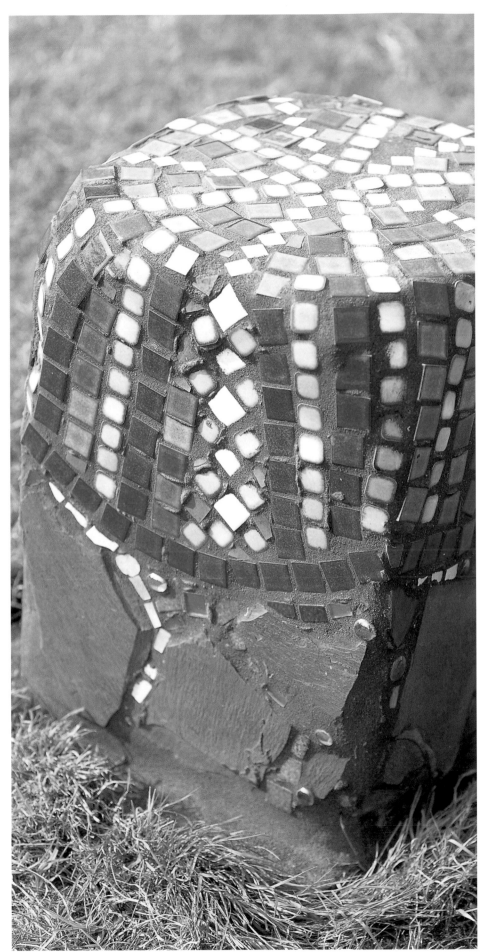

This striking table has been decorated with only bits of broken china and ceramic mosaic tiles, yet with clever colour coordination and a very simple design, it makes an attractive piece of garden furniture.

Shades of Blue Garden Table

You will need

2.5cm (1in) thick plywood
String
Drawing pin (thumb tack)
Pencil
Jigsaw (saber saw)
Abrasive paper (sandpaper)
Wood primer
Paintbrush
Broken china in various colours
and patterns
Tile nippers
Tile adhesive
Flexible knife
Tile grout
Cement stain (optional)
Sponge
Soft cloth

1 To mark a circle on the plywood, tie one end of a length of string, cut to the desired radius of the table top, to a drawing pin (thumb tack), and tie a pencil to the other end. Push the pin into the centre of the plywood, then draw the circle. Cut it out using a jigsaw (saber saw) and sand the edges. Draw your design, adjusting the string to draw concentric circles.

2 Prime the plywood circle with wood primer on the front, back and around the edge. Apply a thick and even coat, and allow each side to dry before proceeding with the next. Allow the primer to dry thoroughly according to the manufacturer's instructions before proceeding further.

3 Using tile nippers, snip pieces of the china to fit your chosen design and arrange them on the table top. Also snip some more regularly shaped pieces, which will decorate the rim of the table.

4 Spread tile adhesive on to the back of each piece of china with a flexible knife before fixing it in position. Cover the whole table with the design, then mosaic the rim.

5 Mix up the grout, adding a stain if desired, then rub it into all the gaps with your fingers. Do not forget the rim. Clean off any excess with a damp sponge, then leave to dry. Polish with a dry, soft cloth.

The combination of colours and the simple design of this mosaic table create a striking piece of furniture. The table can be used outdoors in good weather, but is not completely weatherproof.

Flower Garden Table

You will need

2.5cm (1in) thick plywood sheet

String

Drawing pin (thumb tack)

Soft dark pencil

Jigsaw (saber saw)

Abrasive paper (sandpaper)

Paper

Masking tape

Large sheet of tracing paper

PVA (white) glue

Paintbrush

Vitreous glass mosaic tiles: off-white, light verdigris, dark verdigris, moss, gold-veined verdigris, gold-veined green

Tile nippers

Tile adhesive

Flexible knife

Soft cloth

Tile grout

Grout spreader

Sponge

1 Follow the instructions for the Shades of Blue Garden Table (page 92) to cut a circle from the plywood. Draw a large, rounded petal shape, with half a pointed petal on each side, on paper. Enlarge it on a photocopier until it is the right size for the table top. Then make four copies and stick them all together, so that you have five rounded and five pointed petals. Now trace the design on to tracing paper.

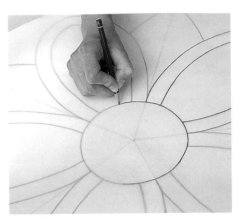

2 Turn the tracing paper over so that the pencil lines are facing down. Place the paper on top of the piece of plywood, and draw over the lines of the design with the pencil to transfer the marks to the plywood.

3 Seal the board with diluted PVA (white) glue, making sure you seal the edge of the plywood as well.

4 Using the tile nippers, cut the glass tiles into halves and thirds so you have a variety of widths. Make a small pile of each colour and save some whole tiles to cut into wedges later. ▶

5 Using a flexible knife, spread tile adhesive over one area at a time, approximately 3mm (⅛in) deep. Select off-white, light verdigris, dark verdigris and moss-coloured tesserae, and press them into the tile adhesive, leaving a tiny gap between each piece for the grout to be applied later. Wipe away any adhesive spillages immediately with a cloth.

6 Fill in the area inside the ring with the gold-veined verdigris and gold-veined green tesserae. In order to achieve a neat finish in the centre of the design, nibble the tesserae into wedge shapes.

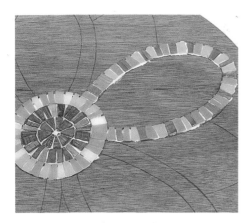

7 Stick down the outside rim of one of the rounded petals, using the light verdigris, dark verdigris and gold-veined verdigris tesserae.

8 Fill in the rounded petal with the light verdigris, dark verdigris, gold-veined verdigris and gold-veined green tesserae, nibbling them to fit neatly within the rim of the petals. Repeat for the other rounded petals.

9 Fill in the pointed petals with the gold-veined verdigris, gold-veined green, light verdigris and dark verdigris tesserae.

10 Fill in the area between the flower design and the edge of the plywood with the off-white, light verdigris and moss tesserae. Leave to dry for a day.

11 Push tile grout into all the cracks between the tesserae using a grout-spreader. Wipe any excess grout off the table top and edge with a damp sponge, then leave to dry.

12 When the table top is dry, turn it over on to a protected surface and spread the base evenly with some tile adhesive in order to seal it. When it is dry, turn the table back again and polish the surface with a dry, soft cloth.

This simple table top has been transformed with a shell mosaic to make a piece of furniture that would be perfect for a patio or conservatory. The symmetrical arrangement of the shells makes an eye-catching design.

Shell Table

You will need

50cm (20in) diameter chipboard
(particle board) table top
Ruler
Pencil
Protractor
Pair of compasses
PVA (white) glue
Paintbrushes
Assortment of shells from old
necklaces or from the beach
Tile nippers
Tile grout
Grout spreader or small palette knife
Flannel (washcloth)
Drill and mop attachment or soft cloth
Emulsion (latex) or watercolour paint:
pale blue-green and pale ochre
Pale blue-green colourwash

2 Using PVA (white) glue and a fine paintbrush, stick a scallop shell to the centre of the table. Glue pink shell pieces from an old necklace inside the starfish shape and surround the starfish with a circle of small snail shells.

3 Break up a sea urchin into tesserae using tile nippers, and glue them in a circle outside the snail shells. Glue ten scallop shells around the edge of the table top, spacing them evenly. Fill in the gaps between the them with mussel shells. Glue cowrie shells in arches between the scallops.

1 Using a ruler, pencil, protractor and a pair of compasses, draw a geometric pattern on the table top, following the one shown here or using a design of your own.

4 Glue a limpet shell in the middle of each space in the inner circle. Fill in the spaces around the limpet shells in between the legs of the starfish with small cockle shells.

5 Fill in the remaining spaces on the table top with an assortment of small shells arranged in a regular pattern.

6 Starting in the centre and working on only a small area at a time, spread tile grout over the surface of the mosaic. Use a grout spreader or small palette knife to press the grout into the gaps. Work the grout into the gaps and smooth the surface with a little water.

7 Press firmly with a damp washcloth to impact the grout around the shells. Rub the flannel over the shells in an outward direction to remove any grout from the surface of the shells.

8 Repeat steps 7–8 until you have grouted the whole mosaic. Leave to dry for several hours, then polish with a mop attachment on your drill or with a soft cloth.

9 Paint the grouting with diluted emulsion (latex) or watercolour paints: pale blue-green for the inner circle and outer edge, and pale ochre for the midway band. Apply several coats of pale blue-green colourwash to the edge of the table top.

This lovely mosaic table provides a stunning focal point for any room in the home. With its swirling pattern, the mosaic evokes fresh sea breezes sweeping in off the water.

Mosaic Glass Table

You will need

Piece of plywood

Jigsaw

Sharp knife

PVA (white) glue

Paintbrushes

Pencil

Tile nippers

Vitreous glass tesserae, in various colours

Cement-based tile adhesive powder

Soft brush

Plastic spray bottle

Cloths

Fine sandpaper

1 Cut the plywood to the desired shape for your table. Score it with a sharp knife and prime it with a coat of diluted PVA (white) glue. Leave to dry thoroughly.

2 For the table design pictured here, use a pencil to draw a series of swirls radiating from the centre of the table. If you prefer, create your own design.

3 Use tile nippers to cut white glass tiles into quarters, and use different densities of white to add interest to the finished design.

4 Brush PVA glue along the pencil line swirls, then position the white glass tiles on top of the layer of glue, smooth side up.

5 Select your colours for the areas between the white lines. Here, browns and sand colours form the edge while blues, greens and whites are used for the central areas. Spread out your selected colours to see whether the combinations work.

6 Using the tile nippers, cut all of the coloured squares you have chosen into quarters.

7 Glue the central pieces to the table-top with PVA glue. To finish off the edge, glue pieces around the border of the table to match the design of the top surface. Leave the glue to dry thoroughly overnight.

8 Sprinkle dry cement-based tile adhesive over the mosaic and spread it with a brush, filling all the spaces. Spray with water wetting all of the cement. Wipe away any excess.

9 Mix up some tile adhesive with water and rub it into the edges of the table with your fingers. Leave it to dry overnight.

10 Rub off any excess cement with fine sandpaper and finish the table by polishing the mosaic thoroughly with a soft cloth.

Water features, such as fountains and ponds, or outdoor wall panels, are ideal ways of giving mosaic a more prominent role in the garden. The reflective qualities of many tiles make them highly suited to water.

Installations

With the natural affinity between mosaic and water, fountains and other water features are ideal opportunities for the mosaicist to display their skill and imagination. The robustness and strength of colour of mosaic proves an effective counterbalance to the clear, fleeting nature of water.

Mosaic is ideally suited to gardens: it can be varied to suit any setting, its resistance to water means that rain or fountains cannot harm it or dim its vibrancy, and the play of ever-changing outdoor light adds constant interest.

It is best to keep any water feature in proportion. In a small courtyard, it can be tucked into a corner, mounted on a wall or even set in a container.

For a natural look, a mosaic of shells, stone or pebble can form a subtle framework for a pool or fountain, which darkens and gleams where the

water moistens the stones. In a formal garden, you might choose to line the floor or the edge of a pool or pond with a suitable motif, while in an urban garden, a square or rectangular feature with geometric decoration looks good. In a cool, green or white garden, you could install a fountain to create delicate dappled reflections.

Above: Circles of oblong mosaics in blues and sea greens grow darker towards the centre of this pond by Trevor Caley, creating an illusion of depth, while random gold splashes add intriguing glitter.

Left: An elegant mirrored fountain by Rebecca Newnham.

Opposite: For richness, nothing beats gold, whether on its own or as part of a design for a bowl. A collection of water features by Elaine M. Goodwin.

A skirting board or step riser is an unusual and discreet way of introducing mosaic into your home. You can use a repeated design (such as this daisy), a succession of motifs, or a combination of the two.

Daisy Step

You will need

Skirting (base) board to fit the room

Abrasive paper (sandpaper)

PVA (white) glue

Paintbrush

Dark pencil

Ruler

Piece of sacking (heavy cloth)

Selection of marble tiles

Hammer

Tile adhesive

Flexible knife

Sponge

Soft cloth

1 Roughen the surface of the skirting (base) board with coarse-grade abrasive paper (sandpaper), then prime with diluted PVA (white) glue. Leave to dry.

2 Mark the skirting board into small, equally spaced sections. Using a dark pencil, draw a simple motif in each section. Here, the motif is a daisy.

3 Smash the marble tiles for the daisies into small pieces with a hammer. It is advisable to wrap the tiles in a piece of sacking (heavy cloth).

4 Using a flexible knife and working on a small area at a time, spread tile adhesive along the lines of your drawing. Press the broken pieces of marble firmly into the adhesive. Choose tesserae in shapes that echo those of the design. The marble can be roughly shaped by tapping the edges of larger tesserae with a hammer. When each motif is tiled, wipe off any excess adhesive with a sponge and leave to dry overnight.

5 Break up the tiles in the background colour with a hammer. Working on a small area at a time, spread adhesive on to the untiled sections of skirting board and press the tesserae into it. When the surface is covered, use small pieces of the background colour to tile along the top edge of the skirting, ensuring that the tesserae do not overlap the edge. Leave to dry for 24 hours.

6 Rub more tile adhesive into the surface of the mosaic with your fingers, filling all the gaps between the tesserae. Use a flexible knife to spread the adhesive into the edge. Wipe off any excess with a damp sponge and leave overnight to dry.

7 Sand off any adhesive that has dried on the surface of the mosaic and polish the surface with a dry, soft cloth. Fix the skirting board in position.

This decorative work is made with handpainted Mexican tiles, which are widely available. The blue-and-white patterned tesserae make a lively background, and the tree trunk is simply the back of the tiles.

Tree of Life Wall Panel

You will need

2cm (¾in) thick plywood sheet, cut to the size required (adjust your measurements to fit a row of whole border tiles in each direction)

Pencil

Drill and rebate (rabbet) bit

Mirror plate, with keyhole opening

Screwdriver

2 x 12mm (½in) screws

PVA (white) glue

Paintbrush

Bradawl or awl

Small handpainted glazed ceramic tiles, for the border

Tape measure

Soft dark pencil

Blue-and-white handpainted glazed ceramic tiles

Plain glazed ceramic household tiles: green, brown and beige

Tile nippers

Tile adhesive

Soft brush

Plant mister

Sponge

Soft cloth

1 On the back of the plywood, mark a point halfway across the width and a third from the top. Drill a rebate (rabbet) to fit under the keyhole of the mirror plate. Screw the plate in place and prime both sides and the edge of the board with diluted PVA (white) glue. Leave to dry, then score the front with a bradawl or awl.

2 Measure the border tiles and draw a frame to match this size on the front of the board. Draw a simple tree in the centre. Cover the border of the board with PVA glue and stick the border tiles in position, placing them closely together and following the frame line.

3 Use tile nippers to cut the blue-and-white tiles into small, irregular shapes. Glue into place for the sky. Cut brown tiles for the trunk; glue them face down on the board and prime with diluted glue. Cut and glue tiles for the leaves and earth. Leave to dry overnight.

4 Brush dry tile adhesive over the panel, filling all the gaps. Spray with water until saturated. When dry, repeat if necessary, then rub adhesive into the crevices, wiping off the excess with a damp sponge. Dry overnight, then polish with a dry, soft cloth.

This lovely design is inspired by the cool tiled floors in Mediterranean countries. The finished mosaic is covered with a sheet of sticky back plastic and lowered on to the floor in sections.

Lemon Tree Floor

You will need

Pencil

Coloured paper

Scissors

Large sheet of white paper

Black felt-tipped pen

Glazed ceramic household tiles:
various shades of yellow, green and
grey, and white

Tile cutter

Tile nippers

Old plain and patterned china

Black ceramic mosaic tiles

White glazed ceramic tiles

Large sheet of sticky back plastic
(contact paper)

Craft (utility) knife

Tile adhesive

Notched and rubber spreaders

Sponge

Soft cloth

1 Draw sufficient lemon and leaf shapes on sheets of different coloured papers to cover the area of floor you wish to mosaic.

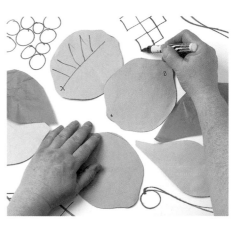

2 Cut the leaves and lemons out and arrange them on the large sheet of white paper. When you are happy with the design, draw in details such as stems and a decorative border around the edge of the design, using a felt-tipped pen.

3 Using a tile cutter, score all the coloured ceramic household tiles down the centre. You may need to practise on some spares to get a straight line. Break each tile into neat halves by applying equal pressure on either side of the scored line with the tile cutter. This will result in a clean break.

4 Using tile nippers, cut these tile pieces into small, equal-size tesserae. Cut up the china in the same way. Also cut up some of the black mosaic tiles, enough to outline each lemon, again into equal-size pieces.

5 Following your paper design, arrange the pieces on a flat surface. To make the lemons appear three-dimensional, place the darker shades on one side. Outline each shape with black mosaic tiles and extend to make a stem.

6 Using tile nippers, cut the white glazed tiles into random shapes. Fill in the background with a mosaic of large and small pieces. When a section is complete, hold the pieces together with a sheet of sticky back plastic.

7 Finish with a border. This undulating border is made of square, yellow-toned tesserae, outlined with rectangular black tiles.

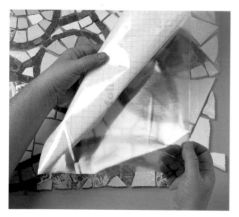

8 Peel the backing paper off the sticky back plastic (contact paper) and lay it carefully over the loose mosaic. You may have to work in sections.

9 Smooth your hands over the plastic to make sure it has adhered to all the tesserae and that any air bubbles are eliminated.

10 Using a craft (utility) knife, cut through the plastic to separate the mosaic into manageable sections.

11 Spread tile adhesive over the floor area, using a notched spreader. Lower the mosaic carefully into the tile adhesive, section by section. Press down and leave to dry overnight. Peel off the plastic then grout the mosaic with more tile adhesive. Wipe off any excess adhesive with a damp sponge, leave to to dry, then polish with a dry, soft cloth.

Gardens offer mosaic artists the opportunity to experiment with more playful wall mosaics. This rather tongue-in-cheek princess design uses tesserae of vitreous glass in vibrant colours that will not fade.

Princess Wall Mosaic

You will need

Brown paper

Pencil

Tracing paper

Scissors

Vitreous glass mosaic tiles in various colours: pink, gold, blue and red

Tile nippers

PVA (white) glue

Mirror

Large wooden board

Tile adhesive

Notched trowel

Grout spreader

Sponge

Abrasive paper (sandpaper)

Dilute hydrochloric acid, goggles and rubber (latex) gloves (optional)

Soft cloth

1 Draw a simple design for a princess on brown paper. Remember that this reverse method means that your mosaic will be worked in reverse, so plan your picture accordingly.

2 Make a tracing of the outline of your drawing and cut this out. You will use this later as a template to mark the area of the wall to be covered with tile adhesive.

3 Using tile nippers, cut vitreous glass mosaic tiles in the chosen outlining colour into eighths.

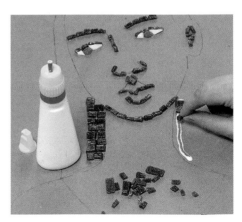

4 Stick these tesserae face down on to the main lines of your drawing using PVA (white) glue. Stick down any key features, such as the eyes and lips, in contrasting colours.

▶

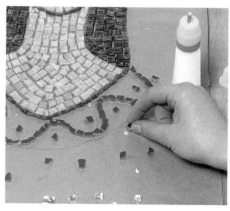

5 Cut pink vitreous glass tiles into quarters. Glue these face down to fill in the areas of skin between the outlines.

6 Cut the mirror into small pieces about the same size as the quartered vitreous glass tesserae.

7 Stick the pieces of mirror face down on to the dress and in the crown.

8 Cut the tiles for the dress and the crown into quarters and glue them face down between the pieces of mirror. Leave the paper-backed mosaic to dry securely in position.

9 Transfer the mosaic to its final location, carrying it on a large wooden board to prevent any tesserae coming loose. Draw around the tracing paper template on the wall or floor. Spread tile adhesive over this area using a notched trowel, then press the mosaic into it, paper side up. Leave to dry for about 2 hours, then dampen the paper with a sponge and gently peel it away. Leave to dry overnight.

10 Grout the mosaic with more tile adhesive, using a grout spreader. Clean off any excess adhesive with a damp sponge and leave the mosaic to dry overnight. Remove any remaining cement with abrasive paper (sandpaper). Alternatively, dilute hydrochloric acid can be used, but you must wear goggles and rubber (latex) gloves and apply it outside or where there is good ventilation. Wash any acid residue from the surface with plenty of water. Finish by polishing the mosaic with a dry, soft cloth.

This richly textured panel is composed of tesserae cut from a variety of patterned china. Motifs are cut out and used as focal points for the patterns; some are raised to give them extra emphasis.

China Mosaic Panel

You will need

2cm (¾in) thick plywood sheet

Pencil

Thick card (stock) (optional)

Jigsaw (saber saw)

Abrasive paper (sandpaper)

PVA (white) glue

Paintbrushes

Wood primer

White undercoat paint

Gloss paint

Mirror plate, with keyhole opening

Drill and rebate (rabbet) bit

2 x 2cm (¾in) screws

Screwdriver

Tracing paper (optional)

Ruler, set square (triangle) and pair of compasses (optional)

Selection of china

Tile nippers

Tile adhesive

Tile grout

Cement stain, vinyl matt emulsion (flat latex) or acrylic paint (optional)

Grout spreader

Nailbrush

Soft cloth

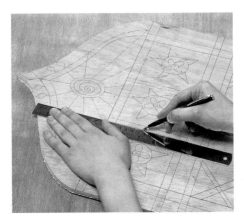

1 Draw the outer shape of the panel on to the sheet of plywood. (If you are unsure about drawing directly on to the surface, make a stencil from thick card.) Cut out around this shape using a jigsaw (saber saw) and sand down the rough edges. Seal one side and the edges with diluted PVA (white) glue. Paint the unsealed side with wood primer, undercoat paint and then gloss paint, allowing each coat to dry before applying the next.

2 Mark the position of the mirror plate on the unsealed back of the panel. Using a drill, rebate (rabbet) the area that will be under the key-hole-shaped opening so that it is large enough to take a screw head. Screw the mirror plate in position.

3 Draw your design on the sealed top surface. If necessary, trace and transfer your original design. Tools such as a ruler, set square and pair of compasses are helpful if your design has geometric elements.

▶

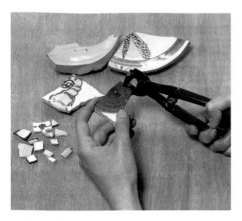

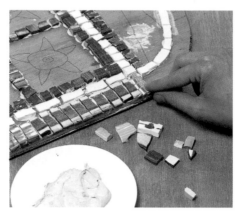

4 Sort the china into groups according to colour and pattern, and select interesting motifs that could be used to form the centrepieces of designs. Using the tile nippers, cut the china into the desired shapes.

5 Using smooth edges cut from cups and plates, press the pieces into the tile adhesive first, then use them to tile the edges of the panel. Use small, regular-shaped tesserae to tile the structural lines of the design.

6 Raise small areas of the mosaic to give greater emphasis to sections of the design by setting the tesserae on a larger mound of tile adhesive. Cut more china and use it to form the patterns between the structural lines. Leave the panel to dry for 24 hours.

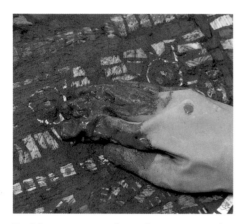

7 If you want the tile grout to be coloured, add cement stain, vinyl matt emulsion (flat latex) or acrylic paint to it. (If this is to be used indoors, cement stain is not essential.) Spread the grout over the surface using a grout spreader. Rub it into the gaps with your fingers.

8 Allow the surface to dry for a few minutes, then scrub off any excess grout using a stiff nailbrush.

9 Leave to dry for 24 hours, then polish the surface with a dry, soft cloth.

This stunning pond is perfect for a small town garden, especially if it is sited near to a patio so that you can admire it while entertaining or dining alfresco on long summer evenings.

Garden Pond

You will need

Paper

Pencil

Outdoor tiles in a selection of greens and blues

Hammer

Piece of sacking (heavy cloth)

Spade

Galvanized metal pond, 1.2m (4ft) in diameter and 60cm (2ft) deep

Sand

Spirit (carpenter's) level

Piece of chalk

Wooden decking

Nails

Jigsaw (saber saw)

Tile adhesive

Adhesive spreader

Tile nippers

Mirror

Glue and glue gun

Tile grout

Flat trowel

Sponge

1 Mark out the design on a piece of paper. This does not have to be to scale, but it will give you some idea of the pattern and colour arrangement.

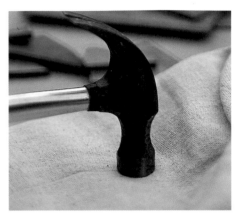

2 Smash the tiles using a hammer and some sacking (heavy cloth). Smash each colour of tile separately and keep the pieces in separate piles.

3 Dig a hole in the ground to accommodate the pond. Bed the pond in with a layer of sand. You will probably have to try the pond in the hole a few times until you get a good fit. Check that it is level with a spirit (carpenter's) level. Using a piece of chalk, mark out the design on the bottom of the pond.

4 Construct the decking by nailing the wooden planks to two cross supports to create a rectangular shape, and then cut out the oval shape with a jigsaw (saber saw). (The picture shows the decking viewed from below.) Lay the oval-shaped piece of decking over the pond, and check that it is level using a spirit level.

▶

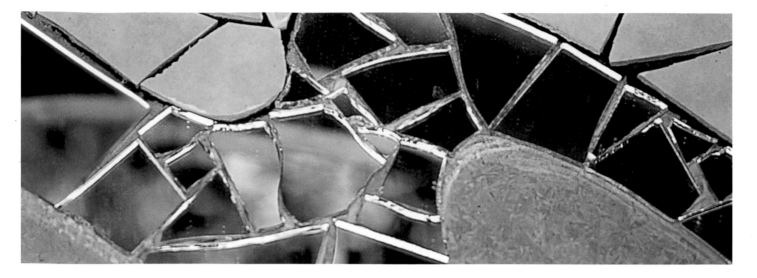

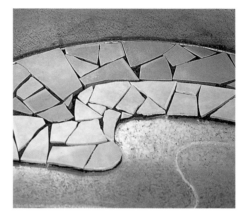

5 Spread a layer of tile adhesive over the first part of the design using an adhesive spreader.

6 Stick the broken pieces of tile along the edge, but within the chalk line. Fill in the inside area. Use tile nippers to get the perfect shape. Finish this colour band.

7 Start on the next colour, sticking down the tiles around the edge inside the chalk line as before. Finish this colour band.

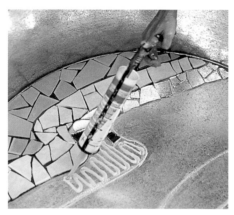

8 Cut up the mirror using the tile nippers. Cover the area for the pieces of mirror with glue from a glue gun, and stick down the mirror pieces as for the tile pieces. Finally, stick down the last colour of tile.

9 Allow the mosaic work to dry for three days. Grout the bottom of the pond with the tile grout, using a flat trowel.

10 Clean with a damp sponge, then fill the pond with water.

This striking water feature is perfect for use outdoors on a patio or indoors in a conservatory. Being portable, it can be brought in and out of the garden and would make a perfect centrepiece.

Fountain Bowl

Circular wooden panel, slightly smaller than the reservoir
Small dustbin (trash can) to act as a reservoir, about 60cm (24in) in diameter and 75cm (30in) deep
Screws
Screwdriver
4 wheeled feet
4 wooden blocks
Drill
5cm (2in) length of copper pipe, 2cm (¾in) in diameter
Hammer
White plastic container
Small pump (4 litres/ 1 gallon per minute)
Selection of vitreous glass mosaic tiles in a range of rich tropical colours
Paper
Tile nippers
Fibreglass bowl with a 2cm (¾in) hole drilled in the centre
Copper spraypaint (optional)
Glue and glue gun
Tile grout
Grout spreader
Sponge

1 Fix the wooden panel inside the reservoir by screwing through from the outside of the dustbin. Attach the wheeled feet to the blocks of wood and screw them to the underside of the wooden panel. Drill a hole near the base of the reservoir for the pump cable.

2 Using a hammer, flatten the piece of copper pipe at one end in order to create a narrow jet of water. Using the tip of a screwdriver, open up the flattened end of the copper pipe slightly to ensure that the water will flow freely.

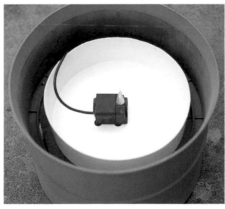

3 Position the white container in the centre of the reservoir, resting on the wooden panel. Add the pump, threading the cable through the hole drilled near the base of the reservoir in step 1.

4 Select the glass tiles in a range of colours to achieve a bold, brightly coloured effect.

5 It is a good idea to test out the mosaic design on a piece of paper first. Arrange the tiles in concentric circles to achieve a pleasing blend of colours.

6 If necessary, cut the tiles into halves using the tile nippers.

7 Spray the outside of the fibreglass bowl with copper paint if desired. Starting at the rim of the bowl, apply two lines of glue from a glue gun, keeping a small gap between the lines.

8 Press each tile firmly on to the adhesive. When the first row of tiles is in place, follow the same procedure for the second row, and continue with each row until you reach the centre.

9 Finish by laying the final circle of tiles around the hole in the centre of the dish. You may have to cut the tiles to fit the final row. Allow to dry. Spread tile grout between the tiles using the grout spreader. Allow to dry, then wipe clean with a damp sponge. Fill the white container with water and place the bowl over the copper pipe.

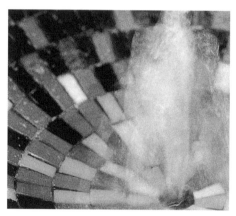

10 Plug in the pump, then adjust its flow rate to create a range of different sounds, from gushing fountain to gentle trickle, depending on your mood.

As the clock must be easy to read, the tesserae are laid in a very simple and precise design. In fact, the primary function of the design, as with any clock, is to draw attention to the position of the hands.

Wall Clock

You will need

Jigsaw (saber saw)

4mm (⅛in) thick plywood

2cm (¾in) thick chipboard

Drill and bits

Clock fittings (battery-operated motor with a long pivotal pin, and hands)

PVA (white) glue

Paintbrush

Strong wood glue

Cramps (at least four) or heavy weights

Felt-tipped pen or pencil

Selection of plain and patterned tiles

Tile nippers

Cement-based tile adhesive

Mixing container

Flexible knife

Shells to mark quarter hours (optional)

Rubber (latex) gloves

Sponge

Abrasive paper (sandpaper)

Soft cloth

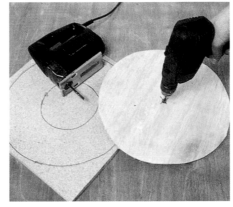

1 Using a jigsaw (saber saw), cut 4mm (⅛in) plywood and 2cm (¾in) chipboard into circles of the same diameter; the circles shown here are 40cm (16in) in diameter. Drill a hole through the centre of the chipboard circle, large enough to take the blade of the jigsaw. Saw a hole large enough to accommodate the clock's workings. Drill a hole through the centre of the plywood circle, large enough to take the pivot for the clock's hands. Prime both pieces with diluted PVA (white) glue and allow to dry.

2 Stick the plywood and chipboard circles together with strong wood glue. Clamp the pieces together with cramps; if you don't have any cramps, use weights such as heavy books. Leave overnight to dry.

3 Draw a circle in the centre of the plywood circle. Its radius must be the length of the longest hand of the clock. Using a felt-tipped pen or pencil, section the face into quarters and use these as a basis for your design.

4 Cut plain tiles into small, roughly rectangular shapes using tile nippers. Mix up some cement-based tile adhesive with water and apply to the edge using a flexible knife. Press the tesserae firmly into the cement. ▶

5 Cut the patterned tiles into small irregular shapes. This design uses three kinds of patterned tiles.

6 Tile the surface within the rotation area of the clock's arms, using cement-based tile adhesive applied to a small area at a time. Take care to lay the tesserae flat, as they must not impede the rotation of the clock's hands.

7 Now tile the border, marking the positions of the quarter hours. Here, shells are used, but whatever you choose, it must not overlap the area where the hands rotate. Leave overnight to dry.

8 Using a flexible knife, smooth cement-based tile adhesive between the tesserae around the edge of the clockface.

9 Wearing rubber gloves, rub cement-based tile adhesive over the surface of the clockface. Make sure all the gaps between the tesserae are filled, then wipe clean with a sponge. Leave to dry for 24 hours.

10 Sand off any excess cement and polish with a soft cloth.

11 Attach the components of the clock's workings. The battery-operated workings should fit into the hole at the back. Fix the pivotal pin through the hole in the centre, then fit the hands over this and secure with a nut.

The ancient tradition of games, paths and puzzles in mosaic gives this simple, strong design an ageless appeal. The background is quick and easy to do, and the swirling design of the snakes uses vibrant colours.

Snakes and Ladders Floor

You will need
Paper
Felt-tipped pens
Tape measure
Scissors
Clear film (plastic wrap)
Fibreglass mesh
Vitreous glass mosaic tiles in various colours and matt (flat) black
Tile nippers
PVA (white) glue
Paintbrush
Patio cleaner
Black cement stain
Tile adhesive
Notched trowel
Sand
Cement
Sponge

1 Draw up a masterplan for the whole board. Play a game on it to make sure that it works. Measure out one of the outside paving slabs to be covered. Cut out 25 pieces of paper to fit the slab.

2 Fold them into quarters and mark out the sections. These are the 100 squares needed for your game. Copy out your design on to the 25 squares of paper using a thick felt-tipped pen.

3 Cover the front of each of the 25 squares with clear film (plastic wrap) and then a piece of mesh, cut to size.

4 Outline each of the 100 squares with matt (flat) black tiles, cut in half. Use PVA (white) glue and a fine paintbrush to stick them to the mesh. Outline the numbers with quarter tiles and the snakes with both half and quarter tiles. Fill in the snakes and ladders with glossy, brightly coloured glass tiles.

5 Fill in the background squares with different colours for even and odd squares. Leave the squares to dry overnight, then turn them over, peel off the paper and the plastic film (used to prevent the tiles and mesh sticking to the paper) and leave until totally dry. Make sure all the tiles are stuck on to the fibreglass mesh, and restick any that fall off.

6 Clean all the paving slabs with patio cleaner and rinse well. Add a black cement stain to the tile adhesive, following the manufacturer's instructions, and apply a thin, even layer to each square with a notched trowel.

7 Lay on the design, one section at a time, allowing for gaps between the slabs. Mark all the pieces clearly and refer to the plan often as you work. Tamp down the squares gently and evenly. Leave to dry completely.

8 Grout the mosaic, using a mixture of sand, cement and water, with an added black stain. Wipe off the excess with a damp sponge and allow to dry slowly.

Acknowledgements/Index

The projects were created by Helen Baird, with the following exceptions:

Michael Ball:
door number plaque (pp. 58–9)
Sandra Hadfield:
decorative planter (pp. 72–3)
Simon Harman:
fountain bowl (pp. 120–2)
Mary Maguire:
shell table (pp. 98–9)
Cleo Mussi:
china tiles (pp. 66–7);
plant pots (pp. 64–5);
decorative spheres (pp. 68–9);
part-tiled flowerpot (p. 74);
sunflower mosaic (p. 93);
star wall motifs (pp. 76–8);
shades of blue garden table
(pp. 92–3); china mosaic
panel (pp. 114–16)
Tabby Riley:
flower garden table (pp. 94–7);
mosaic pond (pp. 117–19)
Sarah Round:
pot stand (p. 61)
Norma Vondee:
sea urchin garden seat
(pp. 90–1); lemon tree floor
(pp. 108–10); snakes and
ladders floor (pp. 126–7)